Dreamcast
internet guide

FKB Publishing Ltd.
Wellpark, Willeys Avenue, Exeter EX2 8BE

Dreamcast Internet Guide
© **1999 FKB Publishing Ltd.**

Sega and Dreamcast are registered trademarks of Sega Enterprises, Ltd.

Author: Paul Bartlett
Websites: Greg Moxham
Editor: Johnny Morrisey
Sub Editor: Ina Oltack
Graphics: Mark James
Contributors: Jade Edwards and Andrew Dixon

Special thanks to: Lulu Pearl, Marc Allera, Steve Wombwell, Rich Lloyd and
the rest of the Dreamcast team.

ISBN 1 902160 24 X

Printed and bound in the UK by The Bath Press.

Dreamcast™

Dreamcast
internet guide

Contents

1-Internet Basics

How does the Internet work? 9

What uses does it have? 9

What sort of privacy do I have? 10

The Main Internet Services 10

Internet Addresses and Domain Names . .11

Common concerns 12

2-Getting Connected

What is needed to connect? 15

Signing Up .15

The Web Browser 16

The Left Menu 16

The Right Menu 17

Bookmarks .17

Troubleshooting 17

The Internet Filter 18

Options 19

3-Dreamarena

What is Dreamarena? 20

Chat 20

Games 21

Lifestyle 22

Shop 23

The Evolving Face of Dreamarena 24

4-Surfing the Web

How to use the Web Browser 25

A little about Web Addresses 26

Links and Buttons 27

Image Maps .27

Error 205 27

Search Engines 28

Multiple Search Engines 29

Online Security 29

Buying Online 29

Media Content 31

The Visual Memory 32

5-Email

What is Email? 34

Understanding Email 34

Sending Email 35

Web-based Email 36

Organising your Email 37

General tips .38

Dealing with Spam 38

Mailing Lists 39

Virus hoaxes 40

Anonymous Remailers 41

A recap of Email netiquette 42

6-Newsgroups

What are Newsgroups 43

Using Newsgroups on the Dreamcast . . .44

Posting to Newsgroups 45

Newsgroup Posting Tips 46

7-Online Gaming

Game Homepages 47

Real Time Online Gaming 49

8-Visual Memory

Downloading Pictures 53

Downloading Game Data 54

9-Your Own Website

Geocities .57

Creating a Website 59

Design Tips 62

General Tips 63

10-Travel

Researching your Destination 65

Arranging a Holiday 66

Airlines 69

Other Transport 70

UK and Ireland travel 72

11-Shopping

Buying Online 74

Buying from Abroad 76

Online Shops 77

Buying via Auction 80

Auction Tips 83

Buying via Newsgroups 84

12-Lifestyle

Employment 85

Dating 88

Food and Drink 89

Website Guide

Index 93

Glossary

Abbreviations & Smileys

Internet Facts

Internet & Game Jokes

1-Internet Basics

During the course of the past ten years, the Internet has been transformed from what was little more than an American University network to an international communication medium. These days most large companies have a Web site, or at least a contact email address. It's now become so popular that once online you may rarely have to use the conventional postal service again. It is not just dull businesses though. The Internet is easily one of the best and cheapest forms of entertainment. From playing games to getting the latest gossip, there are no limits to what the Internet has to offer. You can do your shopping without leaving the house, email your friends and colleagues, find yourself a job, organise your holiday, and get the latest news reports from CNN before they have reached television.

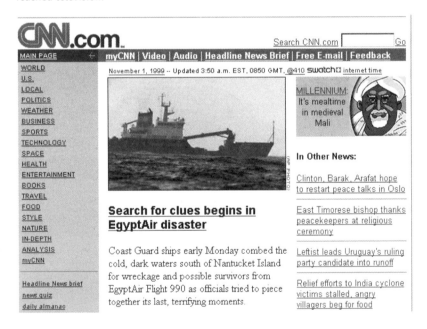

So, what's the catch? Thankfully, there isn't one. It's all out there, and it's nearly free. Notice that word - nearly. Your only problem is the small issue of having to pay the phone bill (which isn't nearly as bad as it sounds, unless you become victim to Internet Addiction

Syndrome). Luckily for you, the Internet is cheaper than it was. You used to have to pay an additional fee to an Internet Service Provider (ISP) to allow you access to the Internet, but these days the ISP will recoup their costs by getting a cut of the money the telephone line providers make. So most Internet access is now free, which is obviously good news. Everyone who uses a Dreamcast to link to the Internet is getting free access. With the phone companies always introducing new call discounts, you can be assured that the cost of surfing will always go down from now on. But what is the Internet, and why should you pay to use it?

In the most basic terms, the Internet is a load of computers that are linked together. Each machine on the Internet is called a server. It's hard to say how many individual networks are a part of the Internet, but one thing's for sure, we're talking millions. The number of individual people that are connected to the Internet cannot be counted, but it's certainly tens of millions, and it's going up so quickly that it's impossible to count. Any estimate will be millions too low within months. The launch of the Dreamcast in the UK has introduced a whole new set of users to the wide and varied wonders of the Internet.

So, you've got all these people that are connected to the Internet. But what are they doing? Well, they're emailing, using the Web, chatting to friends, downloading, and looking at pictures of Britney Spears. The Internet has no boundaries and no regulating body. It's entirely run by the people that use it. It's almost as though it has a mind of it's own. That isn't to say that it is beyond the law of course. If something illegal is being stored on an Internet server in the UK, the police can prosecute the person that put it there. It's not always that easy though, and a lot of things that are strictly speaking illegal (copyright violations mostly) are usually ignored. Smaller copyright violations often serve simply to promote a product. Take, for example, The Blair Witch Project. The huge mass of Websites which sprung up dedicated to it turned an average horror film into an earth-shattering sensation. The same can also be said of South Park - the first 'episode' was originally distributed only via the Internet, and now the Comedy Channel have proven themselves to turn a blind eye to huge amounts of copyright violation as a result.

No doubt you will have heard of couples having met originally on the Internet. Maybe you'll have seen 'You got Mail', with Tom Hanks and Meg Ryan. Well, as daft as it sounds, it can actually happen. Marriages between people who met online happen frequently. Of course, you're unlikely to run into Meg Ryan on the Internet, but you never know do you?

It's very easy to make new friends online, especially through email and chat rooms. You could make friends with someone who lives in your street, or somebody who lives half way around the world. This is particularly useful for people who are shy. The Internet makes finding friends a million times easier. You have no preconceptions about the person you're talking to: age, colour or looks are entirely irrelevant. You can really make a lot of real-life friends, and that's not just hype, either.

Students can find the Internet a God-send. All universities and a lot of colleges offer free access, which should not be ignored. Even if you hate the idea of the Internet, you simply cannot afford to ignore its potential. Whatever you're studying, from Nuclear Physics to Classical Civilisations, there are thousands of sources of information that can help you. It can speed up work tenfold, with no more wandering around libraries hunting for books that have been put in the wrong place or are already on loan. There are even online language translators. They are hardly foolproof, but give fairly usable results, and could help you out of a fix.

It's not just the further-education gang that can benefit either. Any parent who wants his or her children to do well in school should invest in an Internet connection. An added bonus is that no child in the world could possibly complain about being given a Dreamcast - but try unloading a batch of encyclopaedias onto them, and see where that gets you!

If you're thinking of going on holiday, then you can use the Net to research your destination. You can make sure that it's safe, first of all. Then you can check out what other people think of your chosen area, and pick up some hints upon where to go and what to do. Then there's online booking. Flights and Hotels can be checked for availability from the comfort of your own home, and prices are usually cheaper too. Last-minute deals are a breeze on the Internet.

It really is that simple. There's no big deal. The Internet is staggeringly easy to use. Many people are frightened of the Internet because it can appear daunting. Surely nothing so massive can be user-friendly can it? Well actually, it can, and it is.

An important thing to remember is that you should never be afraid to try things out. If you're not sure how something works, guess! Of course, with the help of this book, you probably won't have to.

How does the Internet work?

All of the computers on the Internet communicate in the same language, no matter what kind of specific computer is used. It was developed in the 1960s by the US military, intended to act as the ultimate communication network. The Internet was invented in a time when nuclear attack was almost a reality, so the Internet was designed to be able to survive partial destruction. Previous networks were designed in such a way that if one of the computers was broken, the network fell apart. The Internet is a little more dynamic. If one route to the destination is broken, it'll find another way. As time went by, Universities became a part of the Internet, and the military took a back seat. Eventually, they left it alone altogether. When this happened, people became aware of the commercial possibilities, and things really took off.

The Net is now one of the best ways of communicating with people - cheap, easy and convenient.

What uses does it have?

The Internet has many uses. The main ones to the home user are the ability to send messages to friends and colleagues (email), and the somewhat uncategorisable World Wide Web. The Web (or WWW) is like the world's biggest interactive magazine. There are millions of pages, and anyone in the world can add their own pages at no cost. The range of material available on the Internet is so diverse that if you have an interest, no matter how unusual, there's bound to be people on the Internet who share it with you.

Is the Internet different using a Dreamcast? Compared to using a PC there is not a huge difference. Surfing the Web is very similar. There are a few small bits and pieces not present in version one of the Dreamkey software, but these are likely to be implemented in later versions.

What sort of privacy do I have?

Privacy is limited. Anyone that wanted to trace you having only information gained from your Internet connection would have a very difficult job, but it's not impossible. Bodies such as the police also have an easier time tracking people, but that's another matter entirely. It's not as though your name is splashed all over the place when you connect. Actually you have a reasonably good layer of external protection. You don't need to tell anyone your name, you can keep your exact location to yourself too. It's quite possible for someone to find your country of origin, but that is no huge breach of privacy. Basically, you shouldn't worry about people tracking you down. There is little reason for them to want to. Just be careful about where you put your real name and address. It's not difficult, just a case of using common sense. Never give out your full name, telephone number or address to anyone unless you trust them. Just like in real life (or 'RL' as net junkies prefer to call it).

The Main Internet Services

The World Wide Web

The Web is the world's biggest source of information. Millions of pages of text, pictures, sounds and video. By using a piece of software called a Web Browser, you can easily navigate your way around, either for education or entertainment. Whether it's finding the latest gossip on your favourite soap, or studying for an exam, the Web will be able to help you. To find out more about the Web, go to page 25.

Email

The quickest, most reliable, and cheapest form of communicating with people who aren't in the same room as yourself. Email has taken off to such an extent that it's fast taking over the role of the traditional postal service. Read more about email starting on page 34.

Newsgroups

Whatever your interest, there is probably a Newsgroup where like-minded people can discuss it. Working in a similar way to Email, Newsgroups are one of the best ways of communicating with large amounts of people. More is on page 43.

Downloading

Free modifications to games, special games for the Visual Memory, and grabbing pictures off Websites is all possible with a Dreamcast and a Visual Memory. To read about downloading and the Visual Memory, go to the more detailed explanation on page 53.

Online Gaming

The ability to link up with friends and play either with or against them on your Dreamcast is one of the most exciting possibilities! Check out your options on page 47.

Internet Addresses and Domain Names

This section may be a little confusing or difficult to understand - if you find that it's all a bit too much, don't worry - This is only being mentioned for completeness, and you don't need to have a 100% solid understanding of it to use the Internet.

Every machine on the Internet has it's own address. By this, we don't mean it's physical address. Every machine has to have it's own identity, so that other computers know how to communicate with it. It's best to imagine it like a postal address. When you send a letter (or piece of data), it is sent to the address (or computer) to which it is addressed. If it had no address, it would get lost. It's the same with the Internet.

Usually, these addresses are made up of three parts. Let's take this example:

jackal.anubis.com

Note that there are no capital letters in that address - they are usually not used. In this example address, 'anubis' is the domain name. People pay for their own domain names, which are a combination of one word (or series of words joined by dashes), followed by a three letter suffix. This suffix can be .com (company), .org (organisation), .gov (government) or .net (network). English sites often use .co.uk, and most other countries have their own suffixes. Once you have your own domain name, and a server to which it points (a machine which is permanently connected to the Internet), then you can also assign your own subdomains (in this case, jackal), without paying anything extra.

Computers actually address other machines on the Internet with numbers, not words. They use something called a Domain Name Server to translate these human words into numbers. Thankfully you need to know nothing about this in order to fully use the Internet.

Finally, you should know how to say domain names. You do not say the domain name AltaVista.com as 'AltaVista-full-stop-com' or 'AltaVista com'. The correct way of saying it would be 'AltaVista dot com'. If you're talking about email addresses, then that's easy too. Bob@uk.dreamcast.com becomes 'Bob at UK dot Dreamcast dot com'.

Common Concerns
No doubt you've heard plenty of scare mongering from various newspapers about the horrors of the Internet. In actual fact, unless you're of a severely nervous disposition, there's little to be scared of. However, you should always show some care. These are the main points of concern.

Pornography
There is pornography, and plenty of it. If pornography scares you, stay away from it. It's that simple. It's not as if it's thrown in your face every five minutes whilst researching your science coursework. You could always search for hours trying to find dirty pictures, and then complain about how awful it all is, but there doesn't seem much point, unless you write for a tabloid short of stories. Most pornography sites contain very little in the form of uncensored hard-core action unless you have your credit card handy. Thankfully, the Dreamcast Internet service has a filter which will protect kids from the pornographic horrors of the Internet. This can be turned on or off at your convenience.

Viruses
Computer virii are common on PCs and Macs. They spread around, causing damage to

computer data if people are unprotected. Don't worry though, because it's extremely unlikely that anybody would be able to program a virus capable of infecting the Dreamcast. A general rule is just to be careful when you download software - not really a problem for Dreamcast owners at the moment.

Security

If you have ever watched the X-Files or any of the glut of Hollywood efforts concerning hackers, you'd be forgiven for thinking that hacking into people's machines whilst connecting to the Internet is commonplace. In actual fact, it's more or less impossible. It becomes a problem if you're running a UNIX based operating system, but you don't have that sort of problem with a Dreamcast.

However, there are some serious security issues that affect everybody. One important thing to remember is to be very wary of sending your credit card information over the Net unless you are sending it through a secure server. Secure sites use encryption, in conjunction with the browser, to ensure that any data sent is encoded and safe.

Also, it's important to ensure you never, ever give your passwords to anybody. Many would-be 'hackers' (usually bored teenagers) send emails to people pretending to represent somebody from the ISP. They ask for everyone to send their passwords for 'testing'. No ISP would ever do this, so don't be taken in.

Harassment

Harassment is extremely rare indeed, but it does happen. There are a small proportion of Internet users who are clearly deranged. These pitiful degenerates pick on people for no good reason whatsoever. Usually their threats are limited to emails, which can usually be laughed off and deleted. It can sometimes be a bit more serious however, and the lunatic will need to be taught a lesson. Apparently it's illegal to drag these people from their houses and throw them from tall buildings, but they can be kicked off their ISPs and reported to the police. In many cases, emails can be traced to the sender, even if they use forged addresses.

Don't be discouraged though, harassment is very rare, and if it ever became a problem it can usually be sorted out simply by changing your email address.

So, now you know what the Internet's all about, you'll probably be wanting to connect as soon as possible. Thankfully, that's a lot simpler than you might think. In a few minutes, you could be sending your first email.

2-Getting Started

What is needed to connect?

Everything you need to connect comes inside the box. The modem (modulator-demodulator) is contained within the Dreamcast, and you will also have been supplied with a phone cord and a line-splitter.

If you intend on using the Internet for more than a few minutes a week, then a keyboard comes strongly recommended - it will make typing out those emails much less of a chore! Check your local Dreamcast retailer for details.

Signing Up

Signing to the Internet is simplicity itself, and it only needs to be done once. Better still, it's free, so you won't have to splash out just to test it out.

To begin the process, insert the Dream-Key CD into the Dreamcast and turn it on. Then, simply follow the on-screen instructions. If a blank area comes up in which you have to insert details, then move the cursor over the field and press 'A'. This will open up the virtual-keyboard. Whilst being a bit more time-consuming than a real keyboard, it's easy enough to get used to and simple to operate. You type words by moving the cursor over the desired key and then pressing 'A'. Once you've finished typing, press 'Return'.

You will have to read and agree to the Terms and Conditions, then select to register as a first time user. You will come to the Registration Questionnaire. Right at the bottom of the registration questionnaire, you have to move the cursor over one of the boxes signifying compliance with the terms and conditions. When this is done, make a note of your login-name and password - and keep them safe!

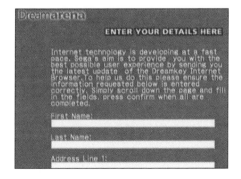

In future, all you have to do to connect to the Internet is type in your password. Whilst connecting, you may hear some strange noises coming from your Dreamcast, but rest assured these are perfectly normal!

The Web Browser

Browsing the Internet on your Dreamcast is a little different to using the Internet on a PC or Macintosh. You'll find that the screen isn't cluttered with buttons or menus, but instead these can be accessed with the triggers (the two buttons situated on the underside of your Dreamcast controller). If you are using the Dreamcast Keyboard, instead of using the left trigger you can use key S1, and instead of the right trigger key S2.

The Left Menu

The left trigger contains the following options:

Home	Go to Dreamarena homepage.
Bookmark	Sort out your favourite sites.
Jump	Type in the URL of your choice and visit the site manually.
Mail	Check out your email options
Chat	Chat to other people connected to Dreamarena
Options	Sort out your preferences.
Disconnect	Disconnect your Dreamcast from the Internet.

The Jump button is your link to the World Wide Web. As the web is separate to the Dreamarena area, you do not even have to enter your password for Dreamarena upon connecting to the Internet. You can just press the left trigger as soon as your name and password have been sent, then enter the address you want to go to.

1 6

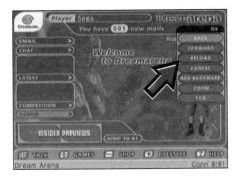

The Right Menu

The right trigger has the following options:

Back	Go back a Web-page.
Forward	Go forward a page (only works if after using the 'back' option).
Reload	Attempt to reload the current Web-page.
Cancel	Stop a Webpage from loading.
Add Bookmark	Add a site to your list of bookmarks so you can easily find it again.
Zoom	Zoom right in on the action

Bookmarks

If you find a Website that you'd like to come back to in the future, you should always bookmark it. Bookmarking will ensure that you never lose your favourite Website. When you make a bookmark (by using the right trigger and selecting 'Add Bookmark'), you are adding to the list already created for you by Sega. Initially, your Dreamcast comes with a number of bookmarks. To view these bookmarks, press the left trigger and simply select 'Bookmark'. You can then scroll up and down the list of Websites offered. Clicking on one will bring up a menu. From here, you can choose to 'Jump' straight to that site, edit the bookmark, or load and save.

Bookmarks are an essential part of your online experience - without them, you'd have to fill notebooks with (often quite large) addresses!

Troubleshooting

There's not as much to go wrong when connecting to the Internet as you might think. With a small amount of luck, you should connect first time. More often than not, problems are easily sorted out. The first thing to do if you cannot connect is to check all of the cables. Make sure that the phone cable is connected both to a phone terminal and to the Dreamcast. This may sound like common sense, but you would be amazed at the amount of problems that can be solved simply by checking connections. The Dreamcast sign-up procedure has been designed to be as simple as possible, and it can usually be achieved in a matter of minutes.

If you still get problems connecting, you would be best advised to phone technical support. There are many things it could be, from problems at the ISP to a faulty modem.

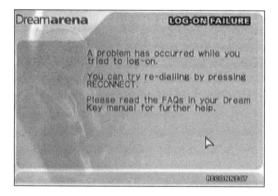

Some Websites may appear to be quicker than others. The reasons for this are varied, but they often mean that the Website you're trying to retrieve is using slow hardware, or is being used by too many people at the same time.

The Internet Filter

For your convinience, Sega has installed a filter on the Dreamcast which won't allow certain Websites to be viewed. These include sites which may contain material unsuitable for children. You may find sites that you would assume you should have access to limited by the filter however. So if you're an adult and you'd like to disable the filter, you will need to do the following:

Access the Options screen on the Left Menu
Select Modem/AT Setup

IMPORTANT Make sure you have your login name and password written down!

Click 'Delete Memory'

Confirm the action by clicking 'yes' at the warning prompt.

Restart the Dreamcast with the Dreamkey CD still inside.

Press start and select 'Restore Me'.

Follow the on screen instructions, inserting your login name and password when required.

Uncheck the box at the bottom of the screen which enables filtering.

There, all done. When you reconnect you'll be able to visit any site freely.

Options

The options screen isn't one you'll have to use very often. It has several options, most of which won't be needed by most people.

Firstly, you can choose to have the audio played in mono or stereo. Then there's the keyboard options. If you've been wise enough to invest in an official Dreamcast keyboard, you'll be able to assign Websites to certain function keys. For example, you could set your Dreamcast to take you to your favourite Website simply by pressing F1, instead of having to select a bookmark or type in the address manually.

Also, if you like, you can change the methods used to scroll up and down the page - you can use either the keyboard, analog controller or the D-pad. There are also several browser options, but these are self-explanatory. It is advisable to steer clear of the modem options, unless you're sure of what you're doing. These include such options as setting a number to dial an outside line and changing from tone to pulse dialling.

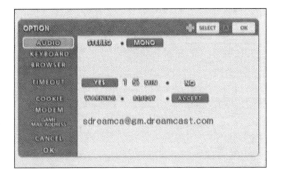

3-Dreamarena

....

What is Dreamarena?

Dreamarena is your home on the Internet. When you connect to Dreamarena you are able to chat to like-minded Dreamcast owners, shop online with your credit card and get the latest international news and sport. Additionally you can read up on all of the current Dreamcast news, games info, hints, tips and gossip. It's also where you collect your email and get online help, should you need it.

Chat

Dreamarena chat allows you to talk to other Dreamcast owners. You can chat about pretty much anything you like, in a selection of different 'rooms'.

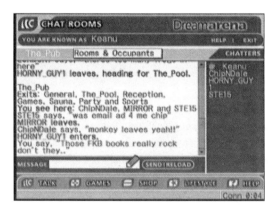

When you first click the 'Chat' button on the page of the Dreamarena (click the left trigger button and select 'home'), you'll be asked to enter a nickname. This can be anything you like, and it's the name that other people in the chat rooms will know you by. You can pick any name you like, but steer clear of anything rude. You may find that your chosen name has already been taken - this is to be expected, because the Dreamarena is very busy. If lots of people had the same nickname, it would get pretty confusing! You can always try using your chosen name followed by a number, or you could just think of something else entirely.

Once you're in the chat room, it's best to just sit and watch for a minute, to make sure

you know exactly what's going on and how things work. Essentially, the text flowing in the left 'frame' is what people are saying to one another. The right frame contains a list of everyone currently in that particular room. You'll notice that above these two frames is a small box stating which room you're currently in. If you click on it, you'll be presented with a list of all the rooms currently available. Each room also has a number beside it, which will tell you how many people are currently in there. If you click on one of the rooms, you'll automatically be transferred there.

The chat frame, on the left, updates periodically with all of the chatter going on in the room. If you type something into the box at the bottom and then press 'send', the page will be updated with your text on it. This also means that everybody else in the room will also see your message.

So, to begin with, pick a room with some people in it, and type 'hello!', or something like that. Then press 'Submit' and see if anybody responds. You'll soon be making plenty of friends!

Games
The games section of Dreamarena is one of the busiest. All the latest Dreamcast releases are covered, with in-depth reviews and the very latest previews.

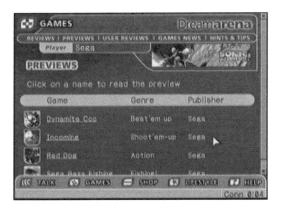

To access the games section, simply go to the main Dreamarena page, and click 'Games', which is in the small box at the bottom of the screen. You'll be taken to the main games index, where you can then choose to read the previews, latest games tips, reviews or news and gossip!

Game news is one of the most popular sections. From here, you can find out the very latest gaming news, before all your mates do! Whilst everyone else is reading magazines which print things three weeks later than they actually happen, you'll be right on the cutting edge.

The hints and tips section may prove very useful if you're stuck on a rather tricky level of Sonic Adventure, or you're just having trouble slapping down your opponents in Ready 2 Rumble.

All of the gaming sections are illustrated with appropriate screenshots and artwork. They are reguarly updated with the latest information.You can even send in your own reviews.

Lifestyle

If you fancy a taste of real life (you'll soon forget what 'real life' is, once you've been on the Internet for a while), you might want to have a quick peek at some of the things residing within the Lifestyle section of Dreamarena. You can read the latest news (world or national), and check out the latest sports information from around the world. There is even a separate football section.

From here, you can also do a search of the Web, using the special Dreamarena service provided by Excite.

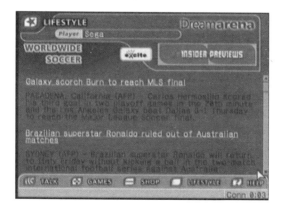

Shop

The Dreamshop has loads of Dreamcast related products that you can buy without leaving your house! The only catch is that you'll need a credit card, so if you're under 18 you'll have to get a parent to order for you.

You can order anything from a new Dreamcast to a keyboard, or the latest games. When you find something that you want to order, you have to click 'Add to basket'. This adds the item to your virtual shopping basket. It's just like the real thing, but without all of those rushing around the shops shenanigans.

Once you've added an item to your virtual basket, you're presented with a form that tells you how to alter the quantity of items you require, and alerts you to the existence of shipping charges. The form at the bottom of the screen is rather self-explanatory. It looks rather like an invoice - it lists the items you require, their quantity, and the sub-total. If you then require to purchase more items at the same time, then you can still look around and add to your basket.

Once you've got everything you want in the basket, you can go to the checkout (click the 'checkout' button at the bottom of the invoice page). Once you've done this, you will be presented with a brief form to fill in. Before you do so, you should read the Terms & Conditions.

After you have filled in the appropriate information, you will have to fill in the invoice and delivery addresses. Then you'll be on to the secure server where you can enter your credit card details with peace of mind. Simple.

The Evolving Face of Dreamarena

Dreamarena is changing all of the time - evolving as user-feedback enables the team running it to get a better idea of the things you want to see. It may be that some of the things you've read in this chapter have changed slightly, but generally everything will work in the same way.

4-Surfing the Web

Surfing the Web has always been one of the most enjoyable aspects of the Internet. It's like having access to the biggest magazine in the world - it's so huge that you can never run out of things to read on it. Whatever your hobbies or interests, there will be someone out these who shares them with you. The World Wide Web can open up a whole new world to you that you never knew existed.

Using Dreamcast, accessing the Web is easier than ever. You can have a quick look around Bill Clinton's Website, or you can have a stroll around the online home of the Royal Family. The world is your oyster, so make the most of it. Just keep your eye on the phone bill!

How to use the Web Browser

To begin with, connect to the Internet and press the left trigger, select 'Jump' and type in:

http://www.excite.co.uk

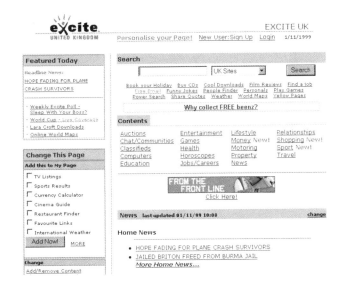

Congratulations, you've just visited your first Website! Or at least, you should have if everything is working correctly. The site you have just been directed to is Excite UK, a famous Web directory. By typing one of your interests into the 'search' field at the top of the Website window, and then clicking 'search', you can find a list of the sites which may interest you. Try the different features on the page and see how it all works.

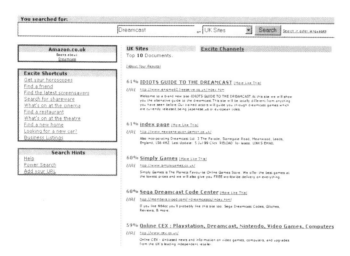

Yahoo is a similar search site to Excite, but it works in a slightly different way. Press the left trigger, select 'Jump' and type in (http://www.yahoo.co.uk). The sites listed in Yahoo are hand-picked, whereas Excite sites are indifferent to the content they include. Excite trawls its way through the Internet, listing each and every site which it comes across. As a result, it has tens of millions of Web pages for you to search through. Before trying Yahoo try pressing the right trigger and selecting the 'back' option. You'll notice that this takes you back to the Excite page. Select the 'forward' option, and you go back to Yahoo. Simple isn't it?

A little about Web Addresses

Now that you have dealt with Web Addresses, or URLs (Universal Resource Locators), you should know how they're made up. It's actually quite simple:

Example: http://www.excite.com/index.html

http://	This shows that the destination is a Web site
www.excite.com	This is the name of the computer (see the previous chapter).
//index.html	The page or file being viewed.

'index.html' is usually the main page of any site. If you go to any site, you will normally be transported to a file called index.html. This is true of top level sites (such as http://www.excite.com/) or sites which reside in an individual folder (http://www.xe.net/currency/). You don't need to type index.html on the end of an address though, since it is the default file sent to you.

You should always remember that Web addresses are case sensitive, (upper and lower case letters are not seen as the same). If you use a different case, it just won't work.

Links and Buttons

The Web is made up of a huge amount of pages, all of which are joined together by links. A link is a word, picture or phrase which links to another file on the Web, usually another page or a picture. On Excite, for example, take the word 'Auctions', under the Contents header. This is a typical link, because it is in blue. Blue text usually, but not always, designates a link. If you hold the cursor over a piece of text, then you can then check at the bottom of the screen to see if it's a link, and if it is, where it links to. When you click on the link, you are immediately transported to the linked file.

Have a play with Excite and using the back and forward buttons. You'll soon get the hang of it.

Image Maps

Image maps are pictures which contain links. For example, you could have a map of the world, and clicking on each country would transport you to a page about that country. Image maps are frequently used on commercial sites, but they aren't used so much on personal Websites, because they are notoriously hard to create without the right software. You can tell if a picture is an image map by moving the cursor around and watching the status bar. If the status bar shows any activity, then the picture is an image map.

Error 205!

It's infuriating, but often you'll follow what looks like a really interesting link, only to be greeted with an 'Error 205' error page. What this means is that the page or file no longer exists at that location. It could have been moved elsewhere, or it could simply have been deleted. There's no way around it, it is just plain annoying. Some search engines will re-visit links on their databases, and remove sites which contain 205 errors - but some are quicker than others.

Search Engines

You should have already visited two of the main search engines in this chapter. They are very important as they are the means to finding what you want on the Net. Without them, you won't be able to do very much. Two of the best are AltaVista (http://www.altavista.com) and Yahoo (http://www.yahoo.co.uk). Yahoo is great in that all of the Web sites are sorted into categories, and are hand-picked. It's like a phone directory, but for the Internet. AltaVista is different in that it's an indiscriminate 'spider'. It automatically trawls the Web, and includes every page it finds in its database. It's the most complete search engine, but it can be harder to find exactly what you're looking for. Yahoo is simple. You type in a word, click search, and it gives you the best categories to look in. If there's a lack of specific categories, it shows you the best individual site matches.

AltaVista is a different story. You type in a word, and it searches its database, bringing up all of the sites that contain that word in them. The more occurrences of the word, the higher up the list the site will be. You can search for both multiple words and sentences easily by using speech marks. So, for example, if you wanted to search for some sites about Eastenders. You could try this search:

Eastenders soap "phil mitchell"

This works quite well, and presents several good sites. No doubt you'd be able to work out some better ones yourself. You'll also notice that AltaVista provides an extra feature. Just above the search results, it says "What can you tell me about the non-U.S. soap opera Eastenders?". By clicking the 'answer' button next to this question, you will automatically be transported to a suitable Web site. Virtually all search engines work in the same way, but most aren't as comprehensive as AltaVista. If you fancy some variation though, you could do worse than try the following - but you may want to turn off the Filter (see page 18) before you try and use them.

Altavista
http://www.altavista.com

Lycos UK
http://www.lycos.co.uk

Excite
http://www.excite.co.uk

It takes time to get the best results from searching. Everybody seems to have their own methods of finding sites, which they all swear by. If you decide to stick with one search engine, always check out the 'Help' pages, which usually have some decent tips on using the service.

Multiple Search Engines

There are various ways of going through all of the search engines at once. One of the easiest is DogPile (http://www.dogpile.com).

It's web-based, and you simply insert your word/s into the engine, and it piles up all of the results from all of the search engines it's aware of.

Online Security

Some Websites ask you pretty personal questions during the sign-up procedure - or they may require your credit card details. In such instances, they will often provide a Secure Server. These servers operate in conjunction with the browser to encrypt data before it's sent. That way, nobody will be able to intercept your personal details. Well, they might be able to, but it'd take them several thousand years of computer processing to decrypt them.

Buying Online

Dreamarena offers plenty of shopping opportunities to buy Dreamcast games and accessories. Dreamshop will also soon be selling a whole range of cool merchandise and other funky stuff.

The Web is more than just a magazine, it's also the world's biggest catalogue. Whatever you need to buy, you can probably find a Website that allows you to get it. A lot of companies are only now waking up to the fact that there's money to be made through selling, and not just advertising things online. The most famous online shop, and the one by which all others are judged, has to be Amazon. It's the world's biggest bookshop, and it operates entirely through the Internet.

Amazon
http://www.amazon.co.uk

Amazon began life in the US, as Amazon.com. They have thousands of books in stock, and can order pretty much any book you like. Their UK Web site now serves English users, but it's always been possible to order from the US branch (if you were willing to pay more for postage, plus taxes). Amazon allows you not only to choose the books you want online, but pay for them online too. This is thanks to the use of a secure server. This encrypts your credit card information (and other stuff too) as it's sent to Amazon. Many people are sceptical of putting their credit card information online, so you have the option of phoning them up with your number if you so wish. Still, if you're brave enough, you can order books without ever leaving your Dreamcast. Amazon claim that nobody has ever suffered credit card fraud after having used their site - and with the level of security provided, this is easy to believe. It's probably safer than giving the information over the phone.

Using Amazon is a simple affair. When you visit the site, you can see a small field into which you type your search words. These can be the names of the author, or the subject of the book you're looking for. When you click 'Go!', you'll be presented with a list of matching titles. You can then pick the ones that interest you. Often they have a further description or scan of the front of the book. If you find a book (or books) that you like, you can just add them to your virtual shopping basket. When you've got everything you need, you have to go to the virtual checkout. Then you just need to fill in some information (address, credit card information), and you're away. You should remember that there are postage costs to pay, but books on Amazon are often quite a lot cheaper than if you bought them in the high street. Price reductions are always stated, so you can make sure you're getting a good deal.

If you'd rather buy videos, then one of the best choices in the UK is Blackstar (at http://www.blackstar.co.uk). They always have a massive amount of videos in stock. You can search the collection online, and every video has its front cover scanned so that you can see what it is you're buying. Each month a different category of videos has 20% off (for example, Science Fiction or Horror). Postage is free worldwide, and they usually ship within a couple of days. They have an absolutely superb range and excellent customer service. Again, they use a secure server to take your credit card details so that they can't be intercepted by malicious hackers.

There are many other online shops, which sell just about everything. Some of the shops based outside the UK will not ship abroad. However, there are plenty of UK online shops and more are starting all the time. Even the supermarket chains are beginning to catch on, and for a small fee some chains will now deliver your online orders. Two established popular sites are:

Unbeatable - Sound & Vision hardware.
http://www.unbeatable.co.uk/

Jungle - Great value CDs, games and videos.
http://www.jungle.com/

Media Content
Many Websites have special media content, such as movies and sound files. Dreamcast can support most of these with ease.

They include:

ADX:	A form of music file.
WAV:	The PC standard for sound clips.
AIFF:	A Macintosh format for sound files.
AV:	Another sound file format.
MIDI:	A format originally designed for synthesisers - file sizes are incredibly small. It acts almost like sheet-music, with the Dreamcast playing appropriate sounds for the instruments described.
MPEG:	MPEG is a form of compression which crunches movie files down to a very small. size. Like Jpeg, but for movies!
Macromedia Flash:	A special form of media. It allows special types of animation and media content to be compressed down to a tiny size - and they always look fantastic.

The Visual Memory

The VM (the Visual Memory Unit that slots into the controller) is a pretty capable bit of hardware. It doesn't just sit there waiting for you to save some games onto it. You can also download game data from the Internet, straight onto the VM. This is a great way of getting past particularly difficult parts in games, and is also useful for sharing your saves over the Internet. Of course you'd have to be a dirty cheat, but then, aren't we all?

Downloading games onto your VM is fairly straightforward. Firstly, go to the appropriate section of a site with VM downloads, and select the saved game that you want to download. Before you download it, you have to make sure that you don't already have any saves for that game on your VM, or the existing one will be deleted! Then ensure you have enough space left on the VM to accept the save. Finally, when you're sure everything's running smoothly, select Yes to downloading the data and the game will download. Then you must select a VM to save the data onto and then wait for the download to finish.

You are able to download mini games that will work on a stand-alone basis on the VM. These games are simplistic but entertaining - and since the VMU is small enough to fit in your pocket, you can take it anywhere!

You can save pictures off the Internet into your VM then bring them up on the screen whenever you like, and also see them incorporated into your screensaver. You can also upload the data you have saved onto your VM into competitions and world rankings. See the Visual Memory chapter for more on the VM.

5-Email

What is Email?

Email has become by far the most popular and productive aspect of the Internet. It was in use long before the World Wide Web, and despite having changed very little over the past twenty years, it's gaining popularity every day.

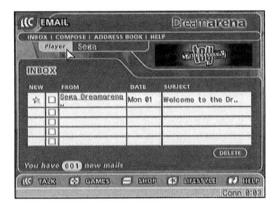

It was initially only used by the military and university students, but now almost everybody with access to a computer has their own email account. Once you try it, you'll know why. Who couldn't find a use for an instant postal service? You click a button, and your message can be in the US within seconds. It is also a lot simpler than you might imagine. Faxing offers much the same kind of service, but it's slower and certainly a great deal more costly. An email can be sent to anywhere in the world, and still cost only a few pence.

It's a great way of communicating, whether it's to friends, business contacts, or loved ones. It's so simple there can be few excuses for not having your own email address.

Understanding Email

Your email address will take the form name@uk.dreamcast.com. Any information on the right-hand side of the @ is the address of the machine upon which your email is stored until you pick it up. You'll have been given your email address at the time of sign-up.

Emails are made up of two parts. The header and the body. The header contains such information as the subject, the date, and the email address of the sender. All of the superfluous information is hidden away, leaving you only with the relevant information (sender, subject and date). The body of the message is the content of the email itself.

To access your email account, press the left shoulder button and select 'Mail'. From here, you can read any emails you have received by clicking on the subject. When you do this, you'll see a FROM field, which tells you who sent you the message, and the SUBJECT field, which usually contains a brief summing up of the contents of the message.

Sending Email

To send an email, you firstly need to know the address to send it to. Once you've got that, you can easily send them a mail by clicking on 'compose', which is on the top left of the screen. You'll need to put the email address of the person you want to write to in the TO field. The format is simply whoever@where.something. You shouldn't include the name of the person in there, just their address. You can put whatever you like in the subject field, and the text of the email should go into MESSAGE field.

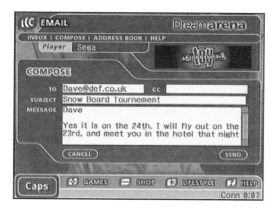

The CC (Carbon Copy) field is for sending messages to more than one person. To use this, simply put the address of the other recipient into the CC field.

With a bit of luck, you should soon start to receive some emails. If you decide to reply to these, you can do so by clicking the Reply button beneath the email. When you do this, you will get the standard mail-creation page, only this time, it won't be blank. The correct address(es) should already be in place, and the mail to which you are replying will be quoted. This means that the previous email will be at the bottom of your reply. You can then either put your new text at the top of the message.

Sometimes, you may receive emails that you would like to share with someone else. Usually these take the form of particularly bad jokes, secrets mailed to you by trusting friends, or business emails that you would like colleagues to see. If this is the case, you can simply forward the mail onto someone else. It's very much like replying, but instead of the email going back to the sender, it can go wherever you like. You can also add your own comments to the top of the mail if you want. To forward an email you must get the mail up on screen, and click the 'Forward' button at the bottom of the message.

Web-based Email
The Dreamarena email system is probably all you will ever need. If you need to access you email away from your Dreamcast you might like to use a Web-based email system that can not only be accessed from your Dreamcast, but also from other systems. You can then check your email from any computer, anywhere in the world. It could also be useful to those forced into using Internet Cafes. It's free, and easy to use.

So, in addition to Dreamarena, what are the best free Web based email sites?

Yahoo! Mail
http://www.yahoo.co.uk
Yahoo offers a good, simple way of running a Web based email address. It can be better in the UK than HotMail, because it's usually considerably quicker. However, you might find it a little more daunting than HotMail if you are a total beginner. In reality, there is not much between the two.

HotMail
http://www.hotmail.com
HotMail, being owned by Microsoft, is very good. It can mess you around in terms of speed at peak times, but you really can't go wrong with it. The HotMail Website contains detailed instructions on signing up and using the service. You may need to disable the Filter (page 18) in order to use Hotmail.

PostMaster

http://www.postmaster.co.uk

This has the major advantage of being UK based, which means speed will almost certainly not be a problem. They have junk mail blocking facilities, and the Web site is beautifully designed, whilst remaining simple to use and quick to load.

There really is little to choose between when it comes to Web based email - but make sure you go for one of the big boys. It could be a disaster if your email account were to suddenly disappear if one of the sites went under. With HotMail and Yahoo, you're almost guaranteed an account for life. You should be warned however that most free email providers will close your account after a certain period of inactivity (usually if you don't check it within a month or two).

Organising your Email

Dreamarena comes equipped with an address book which can be a godsend if you have to send emails to lots of different people (or if you have a particularly bad memory!). The address book can be selected by clicking on the 'Address Book' button whilst in the Mail section of Dreamarena. You can then add addresses by clicking on 'Add Address'. You'll see fields for both the name and address of the person you wish to list. Once you're done, click OK and the name will be added to the list. Then, if you want to send an email to somebody on the list, simply click their name.

General tips

It's important to remember when sending emails that your mail will be read by a human being, and not a computer. Try and be polite and use good grammar. In some cases, particularly when contacting people you don't know, lazy emails can make you look a bit dense. Of course, it doesn't mean you are - but there are times when all you have to go on about a person are their emails - and making a good impression can be important. This is especially true when mailing for business or posting to Newsgroups. Of course, most Internet users are lazy enough, and resort to the common tactic of using strange abbreviations, not using proper grammar and leaving out all upper-case letters. This is fine - as long as the person you're sending them to will be able to understand them and you do not need to impress them.

Dealing with Spam

Spam is a word used to describe junk mail on the Internet. Don't be surprised if within a few weeks of using the Internet, you start to get loads of unsolicited junk in your inbox. You can liken junk mail on the Internet to junk mail that comes through your letterbox. It is 99% of no interest to you and should go straight in the bin, then there is that time you really did need double glazing. The senders are generally (but not exclusively) illegitimate companies or fraud-mongering parasites. There are many different types of spam, but generally, they fit into one of three categories.

The most common is the old "$$$ GET CASH QUICK!" scheme, based around a pyramid scam. They all promise to make you rich just by sending out more emails and sending $5 notes to people, but it never works and is illegal (no matter what the scammers tell you).

Obviously one for the bin.

The second type is of the "See our girls NUDE!" variety. The Internet pornography industry loves to fill your inbox with promises of nudity, filth, and general depravity. Usually, the emails themselves contain little that would upset your elderly grandmother, so they can just be deleted.

The third type of spam is that which tries to sell you something. Do not buy anything from spammers unless you research them carefully or don't mind taking the risk of being ripped off. Of course, if you've bought something from a company and they send you the occasional commercial email, that is an entirely different kettle of carrots. It is not then spam.

One thing a lot of these spam mails contain is a small paragraph at the beginning, which usually reads something like this:

This email message is being sent in accordance with proposed U.S. Federal regulations for commercial email as well as the Washington state commercial email law.
For more information please see: http://www.wa.gov/wwweb/AGO/junkemail/ [Washington State Law].
Sender Information: Scum Industries, PO BOX 666, Nowhere Village, USA
To be removed from future promotions at no cost to you, email bubba@scum.com

Don't be fooled. A lot of spammers include messages like this to make it look as though they are running a completely respectable operation. Be very wary of emailing them and asking to be removed from their mailing lists. This can be just another way to harvest your email address. There is often a computer program sitting around waiting for you to send it a removal email, and when you do, it picks out your email address, and adds it to a list. Then at the end of the day, the spammer has a nice list of verified email addresses that he can sell to some other moron. Some companies have an honest removal option, but you have to decide if they are worth the risk. You may well never receive another email from the same person anyway.

Mailing Lists

If you have a particular interest, you will probably find a mailing list for it. A mailing list is a good way of sharing an interest with like-minded groups of people. In many ways it's a similar concept to that of a Newsgroup (see page 43). You can email a message to the server, and that message will be sent to everybody on the list. They are good for making announcements, or finding out the latest gossip. The amount of subjects range from soaps such as Eastenders & Coronation Street, to computer viruses, system administration, and so on. You can even set up your own mailing lists pretty easily, and for no cost. This is thanks to sites such as http://www.coollist.com, which support themselves by tagging advertising onto the postings. There are more complex ways of managing list servers, but they require that you have access to a machine running a form of the UNIX operating system and the technical knowledge that goes with it.

If you want to join a mailing list, then joining instructions are always provided. However, you should always keep the first mails that you get from the list, which provide removal instructions. You should always unsubscribe correctly from the list, not just send out a message to the entire group asking to be unsubscribed.

Some mailing lists are strictly one-way, and do not allow members of the list to make their own posts. These include, for example, Joke mailing lists (of which several hundred exist). Also, some lists are moderated. This means that all of the messages have to be read by the list owner before they go out to everybody else. This way, rude or inappropriate messages can be cut out before everybody else gets to them.

Find out more information about mailing lists, check out:
http://www.yahoo.co.uk/Computers_and_Internet/Internet/Mailing_Lists/

This section of Yahoo contains simply thousands of lists for you to join, as well as ways of setting up your own list.

Virus hoaxes
Almost a form of spam, virus hoaxes are incredibly common on the Internet. These hoaxes pray on the gullibility and/or lack of technical knowledge of their unwitting victims. They usually claim that there is a new virus on the loose, which travels via email. The claims usually go on to say that if you receive an email with a certain subject, you should delete it at once or risk having your system crashing. All (yes, all) of these warnings are hoaxes, no matter if they say the information was sent out by Microsoft, IBM, or her Majesty the Queen. Of course, being a Dreamcast user you have nothing really to worry about on this front anyway.

```
----- Original Message -----
From: Margaret Jack <margaret.intellica@virgin.net>
To: <margaret.intellica@virgin.net>
Sent: 21 April 1999 17:50
Subject: NEW VIRUS WARNING!!!!!


> Hi,
> If you receive an email titled "It Takes Guts to Say 'Jesus'" DO NOT
> open it.
> It will erase everything on your hard drive. Forward this letter out to
> as many people as you can. This is a new, very malicious virus and not
> many people know about it.
> This information was announced yesterday morning from IBM; please share
> it with everyone that might access the internet.
> Once again, pass this along to EVERYONE in your address book so that
```

One major ISP even sent out one of these ridiculous warnings a year or so back to all of it's customers, and refused to admit that that they had been taken in by a hoax. So, if you've been taken in, don't feel too bad. Even big companies can be ill-informed. If you are worried that someone has sent you a hoax, check out the following site and all shall be explained: http://ciac.llnl.gov/ciac/CIACHoaxes.html.

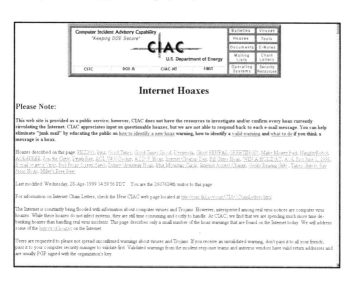

Anonymous Remailers

It's not just spies, terrorists and perverts that want their privacy. There are many acceptable reasons for wanting to keep your identity a secret online. For example, you may wish to

41

make some comments to your boss without him/her knowing who sent them, you may wish to confess to something, without having the whole world know who you are, or you may just want to post something about your fetishes to an 'artistic' Newsgroup. Well, there are many options open to the security conscious among you. The best are anonymous remailers. They are fairly simple in design - you send a mail to the remailer, with a line at the top of the email stating the address of the person you want to contact. The remailer then strips all the information concerning your email address, IP address (your physical address on the Internet - not your email address), ISP and name from the email, and sends the new, cut down version to the final recipient. This way if the recipient tries to trace the sender, he or she would just end up at the remailer, and not at your front door. You are also usually assigned a unique identifying number, so that if the recipient replies, you will actually receive it. Of course, this means that the remailer must hold your real address on file - and if the police wanted to get hold of that information, they probably could. Remailers are usually free, but the classier operations (usually Web based) do charge. Of course, this removes another layer of privacy (they may need credit card numbers, for instance).

Simple in theory but often the opposite in practice, anonymous remailers are the tool of the geeky pros. If you want to learn more about them, then point your browser towards http://www.stack.nl/~galactus/remailers/. This site hasn't been updated for a while, but it's fairly comprehensive, and provides masses of privacy tips, email related and otherwise.

A Recap of Email netiquette
Some of these tips will already have been briefly mentioned in this chapter, but it's worth going over them one more time. The quicker you learn these, the quicker people on the Net will actually treat you with some respect. It may seem harsh, but that's the way it goes.

Firstly, never, ever send out unsolicited commercial emails to anybody. If you do, you deserve all of the abuse and flak you'll get as a result of it.

Secondly, you should never send emails written entirely in capital letters. Capital letters are considered to be 'shouting'. It's more acceptable to type purely in lower-case letters, but it's certainly preferable to use proper grammar and punctuation. This is especially important if the email you're sending has to give a good impression!

Finally, never send or forward 'chain mails' or pyramid scams. Simple really isn't it?

6-Newsgroups

What are Newsgroups?

Newsgroups (otherwise known as Usenet) are the best way of talking to people whom you know have similar interests to yourself. It's best to think of it as a message board. You email your messages to the board, where other people can pick them up and reply to them if they feel like it. Actually, it's a little more complicated than that. There are many thousands of message boards, all of which communicate with each other and share the same information. So it acts as though there was only one. It works using email, so it's pretty simple to get involved in.

There are Newsgroups on every topic imaginable. There are thousands of them out there, and they cater for more or less every interest. When you find one that looks as though it would interest you, all you need to do is 'subscribe' to it. This isn't quite as it sounds - you aren't really subscribing to anything as such, so don't worry. It just means that you can use the group if you want to. So, once you're on board, all you need to do is click on any message you want to read. It will then come up on the screen, and you can either reply to it, or ignore it. You can send your reply to either the author of the posting or the Newsgroup itself. Most people post to the Newsgroup so that their reply can be read by everyone else.

Using Nesgroups on the Dreamcsast

The Dreamcast can't currently access the Newsgroups in the same way as a PC or Mac can. These systems have specialised software (much like email software) which allows them to access the Newsgroups easily and quickly. The Dreamcast doesn't have Newsgroup capabilities at the moment, but you can still access the information in the various groups for via the World Wide Web. To do this you can use the site Deja (http://www.deja.com). It retains millions upon millions of Newsgroup postings from the majority of existing groups - going all the way back to 1995! You can search this huge database of knowledge and find out just about anything you like! Before going into the ins and outs of using Deja to search Newsgroups, let's take a quick look at how Newsgroups work.

The Newsgroup hierarchy may initially seem quite daunting, but it's pretty simple. All Newsgroup names are made up of at least two parts. Firstly they have a top level category name. For example, in the case of alt.test, this would be 'alt'. The Alt category is the anarchic part of Usenet, in which thousands of groups reside. Anyone with the knowledge can create a group under the Alt category, and so the re thousands of them available.

Here are some of the other main categories:

comp	-	Computer related talk.
uk	-	Groups concerning UK issues.
rec	-	Recreational activities
misc	-	Enough said.
news	-	Information about Usenet itself.

If a group has 'binaries' in it's title, then it means that the group is intended for files only. These could be pictures, sounds, movies or any other kind of file, but you won't be able to view any of them through Deja.

Now, let's say you wanted to find out about caring for Dogs. You could load up the Deja homepage (http://www.deja.com), and type 'dogs' in the search field. Click on 'Search', and a list of appropriate articles will be displayed. Naturally, you'll want to narrow it down (a search for 'dogs' comes up with over 30,000 matches). You can see at the top of the page there is a small list of appropriate Newsgroups (called 'forums' by Deja, for reasons unknown) which you can view by clicking on them.

The best method for searching is to use the Power Search option (the Power Search link is always contained in the 'search' box). From here you can narrow the discussion down to the Newsgroup and date. So let's say we used the above search for dogs, which reveals the Newsgroup name 'rec.pets.dogs.breeds'. Now, imagine you wanted to learn about sheepdogs. You could type 'sheepdogs' into the keywords field, and 'rec.pets.dogs.breeds' in the 'forum' field. There are plenty of other narrowing-down options you can use if required. Clicking OK will then reveal all of the posts relevant to sheepdogs. Inserting other words into the 'keywords' field can help to narrow it down even further. It might sound complicated, but it's really very simple when you get into it.

Posting to Newsgroups

You can even use Deja to post to Newsgroups - this isn't something to be taken lightly since it's fairly time-consuming and isn't worth the effort for day-to-day posting. It's best to use if you're really stuck for an answer to an important question, and think that Newsgroups are your last chance, because it is so time-consuming.

Firstly, you'll need to register with My Deja. There will be a link on the main page which allows you to do this. You'll have to fill in a brief form which asks for your preferred username, password and email address. Once this is done, an email will be sent to your email account. You have to read this mail before you can go any further, because it contains the information needed to finish off your registration. Once you've got the mail up on your screen, click on the Web address as indicated. Once that's done, you'll be shown a screen which tells you that your account registration has gone through successfully. Make sure you keep a note of your username and password, because you will need them to log on in the future.

Once you're registered, all you need to do is visit http://www.deja.com/post.xp. From here, you type out your message as if it was a normal email. There is a small pull-down menu which contains some of the more popular Newsgroups that you could post to, but it's almost certain that you'll be wanting to find a more appropriate Newsgroup for your posting. To do this, just click on 'find a different forum' before writing your message. Then just type in a keyword or two and you'll be presented with the most likely groups. Click on the one that seems the most likely, and follow the instructions to post to it. It's highly recommended that you make sure the box which reads 'Send me Deja Tracker emails when someone responds to this message' is ticked. This is because, without it, you'll find it very difficult to track replies to your message. This way, Deja will send on any replies to you via email.

Newsgroup Posting Tips
Never send commercial postings to Newsgroups. You won't be thanked for it, and it can get you into trouble! This is doubly true for 'Make Money Fast' pyramid scams.

Always be polite! Never get drawn into a nasty argument. The Internet's full of sad bigots, racists and other assorted scum. Don't humour them by joining in an argument, it's just a waste of your phone bill.

Try to use proper English & spelling as much as possible. Nobody likes to sit down and spend ages trying to work out what somebody is trying to say!

Learn the slang, abbreviations and smileys! This is very important to avoid misunderstandings. You'll find these terms at the end of the book.

7-Online Gaming

Dreamcast can use the internet for its games in two ways. Firstly certain Dreamcast games have homepages. These contain downloads of extra code for the game, bulletin boards where you can send and read game information, and online competitions. Secondly games can be played against other users logged on to the internet in real time.

Game Homepages

Sonic Adventure has an evolving homepage that you can access by loading Sonic Adventure and selecting Internet from the title page.

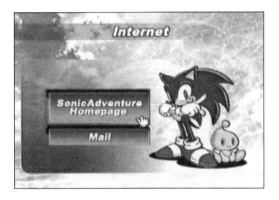

When you first enter the Sonic homepage you will be on the News Updates screen. This is the page that keeps you up-to-date with Sonic on the Internet. Information about downloads, competitions and tips are all provided here. You also have the option to view previous news in the Update Archive. Here all the past news is kept so you do not have to worry about missing anything.

Chat is unfortunately currently only available in America, but it is no great loss as the Boards section does the same thing in a better way.

The community section of the site is where you can view the world rankings and upload your VM saves to enter them. This is also where you can download updated code for the game. This is covered in the next chapter, the Visual Memory (VM).

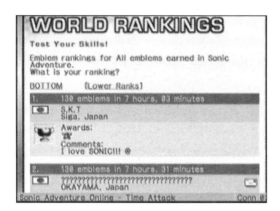

The Boards section of the site allows you to send and view information under different sections, depending on how advanced you are on the game. It is the online community for Sonic Adventure. The Boards are very similar to Newsgroups which are discussed in chapter 6.

If you are having trouble with any aspect of the Sonic homepage then select the Support page and you will get information about how to use the site, how to use your VM with the site and other general help.

Buggy Heat also has its own online homepage. You access it from the main Title page of Buggy Heat. It allows you to rank yourself against everyone else's times on all the tracks and difficulty settings and upload and download AI drivers. It also has a help guide to give you tips on the game.

Although not as involved or exciting as the Sonic site at launch, the Buggy Heat site is

due to be updated with new features being added in the future.

One of the features expected at Buggy Heat online are the competitions that the Sonic site has. At present you are able to upload your best times from your VM onto the site, but in the future you should be able to use this feature to win prizes.

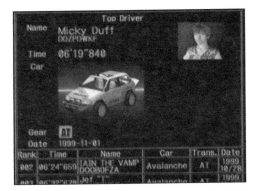

The most interactive and exciting part of Buggy Heat online is the AI driver data. By selcting AI ranking you can view and download other players AI data. Then with this safely stored in your VM you can race against the downloaded AI driver in the VS game. Downloading is covered in more detail in the following VM chapter.

More games will have online homepages in the future, allowing you to compare your skills with other players, discuss tactics, find tips, enter competitions and download additional code.

Real Time Online Gaming

The other way the Dreamcast interacts with games and the Internet is by competing in real time against other players. None of the launch games for the system have this option, but the next generation of games will start to come ready for real time online gaming.

For a long time games have provided a standard two player option which works via a split screen mode, but it's only been within the past few years that games have been developed which allow players to connect with many others over the Internet. There are plenty of possibilities, and you do not need to just compete alone, you can do so in teams.

One of the earliest major (and certainly most popular) online games was Quake. Everyone should have heard of it, it followed on from the famous first-person shooter Doom. The original Quake is ancient history now. It brought huge attention to the world of real time online gaming, but better games are taking over its crown.

The Dreamcast is ready to open up the world of real time online games to everyone. By Winter 2000 it will be fairly standard for Dreamcast games to have online multi-player options. Online football, basketball, and driving games are already in development for release in 2000. The first online games will be available around Easter 2000, with more and more new releases having the option from then on.

Dreamcast online games will introduce features like online ranking of players. Up to several hundred thousand people will be able to be ranked against each other in a true battle to be the best online player. Other innovative online features are expected to develop as the Dreamcast is the first system of its type. All Dreamcast internet users have a Dreamcast email address that can be esily reached by Sega. This allows Dreamcast owners to be more in control. It is very possible that Dreamcast users will be polled on online gaming issues in the future, giving you a say in your system.

Some of the first big online games expected to appear on the Dreamcast include Chu Chu Rocket, Baldur's Gate, and Halflife.

Chu Chu Rocket is a title currently in development by the wizards at Sonic Team. It is a bizarre game that involves guiding as many mice as possible into your rocket. It is being designed to have an easy to grasp, hard to put down quality. What we can expect is an addictive romp due out for Easter 2000.

Baldur's Gate is a likely early online game release. This hugely popular roleplay game has already been a monster hit on PC and is certain to be a Dreamcast hit with anyone

who wants a more involving challenge.

Half-Life is one of the most popular online games and is being developed for a Dreamcast release sometime during the year 2000. There are already a huge number of Websites devoted to Half-Life from its success on the PC. To get some idea of what you can expect on the Dreamcast, and the fan following the game already has, you can look at some of the current Websites:

http://www.halflife.org, http://www.planethalflife.com, http://www.halflife.net

Real time online games are the most exciting games development in the past few years.

The Dreamcast is the first console to harness the potential of the Internet for such a purpose. It also has an unseen before level playing field. The fact that every Dreamcast is identical ensures that every online gamer has an equal opportunity to win. PC gamers do not have this luxury.

8-Visual Memory

The Visual Memory (VM) can be used to store images from the Internet, download extra data for games, download its own games, and upload data to the Internet.

Downloading Pictures

You can download images from anywhere on the Internet and store them in your VM. In order to download move the pointer over an image on a website and press keys X and A at the same time.

You will be asked if you wish to save the image. Selecting Yes will take you to the Option Screen where you need to select the VM to download onto. Once selected the image will download onto your VM which will take a few seconds. The picture can now be brought up on the screen at any time by selecting File on the Right Menu and finding it on your VM. The image will also now be incorporated into the screensaver, (the image that comes up when you leave your Dreamcast idle).

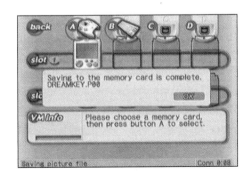

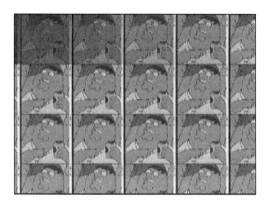

Once saved on your VM an image will be used in your screensaver.

Downloading Game Data

Dreamcast games with their own homepages on the Internet have the capability of storing data for you to download. Already covered briefly in the previous chapter, both Sonic Adventure and Buggy Heat allow you to download to your VM.

The Sonic Adventure homepage is designed to allow lots of different downloads to be put on the site reguarly. By looking at the News Updates you can see what downloads have been put on the site, and what to expect to appear soon. Downloads include special levels to tie in with seasonal events, and to be used as the basis for competitions.

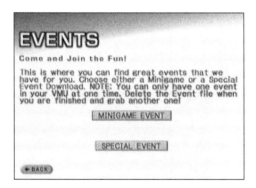

To download from the Sonic site first find out in Updates which part of the site the download you want is in. Then click on the download you want and you will be asked if you want to download the file. Select Yes and you can see the data download into your

Dreamcast. This may take a little while.

Once downloaded you need to select a VM to store the data on, then watch the information copy onto the unit.

The VM is also the way you upload your scores and achievments onto game websites. In Sonic you can take your save and upload it into the World Rankings. If you are good enough to come near the top you could be in a position to win prizes. Each competition explains how to upload from the VM, which will usually involves holding a couple of buttons on the 'Select a file' menu in the game.

Buggy Heat allows you to download and upload your AI data onto the homepage. This is a great way to pitch yourself against other players. Select 'AI ranking' and click on the player you want to download the AI from. You will now be asked to confirm the download. Select yes and you will be able to store the data on your Visual Memory.

You can also upload your AI onto the Buggy Heat homepage. To do this you need to select Entry on the AI ranking option. You then have to fill out a short questionnaire and select Go to send your data to the site.

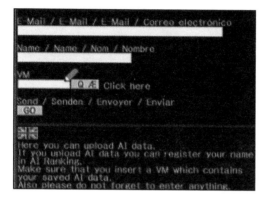

9-Your Own Website

••

When you've been surfing for a while, you might decide that you'd like to add your own contribution to the World Wide Web. Thankfully, creating a Web site is very easy. You can create a Web site about almost anything. It could be about your favourite band, your favourite author - or it could be more general. A site containing film or music reviews, for example - it's up to you.

Because you're using a Dreamcast, you won't be able to add pictures to your Website unless you also have access to a PC or Macintosh, but putting up a text-based Website is easy enough!

Geocities

Geocities (http://geocities.yahoo.com) is where we'll be storing our homepage in this example. It's the most famous free-Web space provider in the world, with millions of satisfied users. You get 15 Megs of disk space, and a reliable service. All Web sites are put into categories and sub-categories, which means that your URL can be very long indeed. A free email account is also supplied.

You need to sign up with Yahoo/Geocities before you can create your Website. Select the link for this on the main Geocities page. You need to enter a little bit of personal information, and choose a login name and password. Once you've done all this, you should go back to Geocities. From here, choose the Yahoo! PageBuilder - a link is provided near the bottom of the page.

The first thing to do once you have logged in is to choose a Neighbourhood in which to put your site. You have to pick something appropriate, so if you're doing a page about animals, you would choose the terribly-named 'Petsburgh'. After deciding on a Neighbourhood go and check your email. You should have an email from Geocities which explains how to create your site. Read it through to make sure you understand how it all works.

You are now ready to go back to the main Geocities page and select 'Edit pages'. You will be given the choice between 'beginners' and 'advanced'. You need to select 'advanced' because the beginner mode will not currently work on the Dreamcast due to the way Java is used on the site.

This is where is starts to get mildly tricky. The next page shows a list of the files in your account. Now, there should only be one file - index.html. That's your Web page. So, tick

the box next to it and click 'edit'. The next thing you know, the HTML of your Website will be displayed in front of you. Select all of it with the controller, and delete it all. You don't need that - you'll be putting your own HTML in there! But what on earth does it all mean?

Creating a Website

This is the difficult part - learning HTML. This book couldn't possibly instruct you on the ins and outs of Website creation (that is a whole other book)- but we can give you enough information to create a reasonably decent site.

HTML (Hypertext Markup Language) is not a programming language, just a way of formatting text. An HTML document is nothing more than a plain text file.

An HTML document contains the text that you want on your page, interspersed with lots of control codes. The Web browser will be looking for these control codes when it displays a page - otherwise it will be shown as a simple page full of text. These control codes have to do everything, from making links to starting a new paragraph.

Control codes (from now on known as 'tags') are always contained within angle brackets (the < > things). These tags are inserted in and around the text, and it can be quite confusing at first. It isn't that bad however, and once you understand what each tag does it will become very clear.

Tags are usually used in pairs. For example:

<b> this text would be bold </b>

The <b> tells the browser that all following text is to be displayed in bold. The </b> tells the browser that the bold text ends at that point.

That much is easy to grasp. Here are some other simple tags which work along very similar lines:

Start Tag	Action	End Tag
<i>	Present all following text in italics.	</i>
<u>	Underline all following text.	</u>
<p>	Start a paragraph	</p>

`<h1>`	Header text - different numbers make different sizes.	`</h1>`
`<html>`	Put at the start (and at the end) of each HTML document.	`</html>`
`<center>`	Puts all text in the centre of the window.	`</center>`

So you can see how tags work at their most basic. Perhaps the best way to illustrate how the other tags would be to do so in the context of examining a simple piece of HTML. Before examining some text you should know that HTML documents don't have to be formatted well - for example:

This is a line of text.
`<br>`

...would work in exactly the same way as this:

this is a line of text.`<br>`

The extra line in the first example would be ignored. You could do your entire page as one big block of text if you wanted to, the results would still be the same.

Most people like to space things out a bit to make the pages easier to edit and follow. This has been done to some extent in the following..

The following is a simple example. First, let's take a look at the finished page - to see what it is we're working towards.

Bob's site

Hi! My name's Bob, and on this site you can read all about my fascinating life story, read my CV, or learn about my fantastic hobby - putting things on top of one another

My favourite links:
Dreamcast Europe! Visit the homepage of my favourite console!
Lycos.com Try this search engine when you're bored of reading about me!

Email me

— html begins—

<html> **[designates the beginning of the HTML]**
<BODY BGCOLOR="#FFFFFF"> **[sets the background colour to white. The #ffffff part is a hex value. #000000 would be black]**
<center> <h1> **[centre the text and make it larger (header) text]** Bob's site </h1>
</center> **[turn off the centering and header sized text]**
 [change to a new line]

 [add another new line, to space things out a bit]
Hi! My name's Bob, and on this site you can read all about my <a href = "lifestory.html">
[designate the start of a link - all following text will be a clickable link to another page - lifestory.html] fascinating life story</a> **[end the link]**, read my<a href = "cv.html">CV</a>, or learn about my fantastic hobby - <a href = "hobby.html">putting things on top of one another.</a>.

<b>My favourite links:</b>**[make this small heading bold]**
<a href = "http://www.dreamcast-europe.com">Dreamcast Europe!</a>. Visit the homepage of my favourite console!
<a href = "http://www.lycos.com">Lycos.com</a>. Try this search engine when you're bored of reading about me!.
.

<center><a href = "mailto:bob@interesting.org">Email me</a></center>

</html>
—ends—

Although that Website would win no design awards, and certainly no awards for the quality of the HTML code, (an HTML expert would probably be able to find a dozen or more faults with the HTML), the point is that as long as it works, that's all that matters. Most Websites are amateur efforts, and hardly anybody knows HTML well enough to do a perfect site. There are all manner of rules that you are expected to follow when writing HTML, but at the end of the day, if the site works, then they are rather unimportant.

There are more advanced topics such as frames, tables or Javascript. You can find out about them either by using a search engine to find informative Websites.

Design tips

It's no good learning HTML if you're going to produce the sort of page that nobody will want to read. The design of a Web site is often directly related to it's success or failure. There are handy tipsto help you get ahead in the Web design stakes.

Be sensible with the colours that you use. Don't go mad with reds and yellows!

If you also have access to a computer and the facility to upload images to your Website, don't be tempted to fill the page with huge photos - nobody likes a site that takes ages to load. On a similar note, be wary of including MIDI files on your Website - too many people do it already! What this means is that when the Web page loads, it will play an awful plinky-plonky little tune. To many this becomes absolutely maddening, and many surfers refuse to re-visit sites that contain such annoyances. You have been warned!

Use frames wisely. Many people use too many frames, and it gets confusing. You're probably confused already, since we haven't covered frames in this chapter - but don't worry, you'll soon pick it all up! You can search on Yahoo (http://www.yahoo.com) for HTML help sites!

When linking to an external site within a frame, it is best that a new browser window is opened for the link. Don't let the external site load into one of your frames, it is generally not liked.

Use small text. A page full of huge text is very hard on the eyes! If you use a background image try to find or create one that's in greyscale, and make sure the brightness of the image is turned up, and the contrast is turned down. That way it can still be seen, but it is never darker than the text, and exhibits a very nice 'watermark' effect, rather than making your eyes hurt.

Don't go overboard on the amount of fonts you use when creating images for your site. Two different fonts are usually more than enough.

General tips

If you think your site is worth it, then submit it to as many search engines as you can. Go to the homepage of each search engine to find out how to add your site to it. This is the only way you're going to get any hits! Particularly important is to add your site to Excite (http://www.excite.com), AltaVista (http://www.altavista.com) and Yahoo (http://www.yahoo.com).

Make sure your site is going to interest people. Too many people put up a dull site which lists their friends, hobbies and their pet's names. Nobody will want to read that stuff, unless they fancy you!

Be careful about breaking copyright laws. Several companies, including Sony and 20th Century Fox have proven their ability to bully Website owners into removing things such as song lyrics and pictures from their Websites. This may not be commendable behaviour on the part of the companies involved, but unfortunately if it came to a court case, they are likely to win!

Don't link to anything that contains something that is illegal. It's been proven in court that linking to an illegal Website can be considered to be the same as 'publishing' the material! This may be outrageous, but that's the way it goes.

Including a guestbook can often help you out. People can leave feedback, be it either encouragement of constructive criticism. You can get a free Guestbook from http://www.alxbook.com/. In a similar vein, try and encourage people to email you with their comments.

Starting a small mailing list can help to keep your visitors updated on the latest news. Go to http://www.listbot.com/ for a free one.

10-Travel

Arranging a holiday has never been easier. You don't have to deal with pushy or ignorant sales staff, andall the information that you need can be found online. This includes safety warnings and tourist information. The ability to communicate with fellow travellers also provides a unique method of investigating your choices. Arranging insurance is also much easier online, and less time consuming.

Conventional travel agents are all very well, but the advice that they offer is rarely impartial and comparing prices & weighing up the pros and cons can be a nightmare. The Internet makes this all so much easier. There are forums where opinions and information can be exchanged with fellow travellers, and there are many Websites where the very latest prices for a huge number of flights and package trips can be obtained in seconds for instant comparison. No hard-sell, no pressure to make an instant decision. Once you've arranged a holiday over the Internet, you'll never want to step into a travel agent's again.

One of the new breed of travel sites in the UK is Microsoft Expedia. (http://www.expedia.com)

Linked with MSN, the Microsoft Online Content Provider, Expedia offers the UK traveller a wealth of information which can prove invaluable if you are planning a trip. Even if you don't plan on booking online, it can still help to get all of the latest prices and information before you go to the Travel agents. Get yourself some ammunition before you face the people who are out for your money!

Expedia isn't the only Website that exists for this purpose either. There are plenty of others, each of which varies in terms of the quality and quantity of information provided.

Researching your destination

Using the Internet, you will find a wealth of information and guides to virtually anywhere on the planet. Possibly one of the best places to find all the information is the World Travel Guide online (http://www.wtgonline.com/navigate/world.asp). This comprehensive site provides practical information, including travel details, health and safety, visa information and brief guides to every country in the world. Rough Guide (http://travel.roughguides.com), Lonely Planet (http://www.lonelyplanet.com) and Lets Go (http://www.letsgo.com) all have lots of information on their websites, although nowhere near as much as they put in their books.

Almost every major town and city around the world has at least one of its own tourist Websites featuring special events, guides, maps and a whole host of other useful information. The standard of these sites varies, although they are generally very good. Most can be found with a fairly simple search using Excite.

If you are looking for a specific type of holiday then using a search engine will generally provide you with some good sites to help you research further. Backpackers should take a look at Backpack Europe (http://www.backpackeurope.com), which contains masses of information and links. Skiers should visit Ski.com (http://www.ski.com), which provides news, equipment information and details of resorts throughout the world.

Arranging a Holiday

Travel is just one of the latest areas that the Microsoft empire has conquered, and with great success. Expedia UK (http://www.expedia.co.uk) is a comprehensive site that offers varying methods of finding a suitable holiday and booking it online. It's quite a smart site, and is also very easy to navigate. When you visit the site, you will notice that a large part of the front page is taken up by the Flight Finder. This is a search engine that allows you to search a database containing all of the flights leaving from a number of the UK's main airports (Gatwick, Heathrow and so forth), both by destination and departure date. There are also fields for selecting how many adults will be on the trip, and the results can be sorted either by price or by airline. This is pretty simple to operate. If you find an offer that is too good to refuse, you can book the flight online. You will need your credit card details handy, but you do not worry about sending your credit card details over the Internet, the site uses secure encryption so that personal information sent to Expedia cannot be intercepted. You could quite easily find and book the flight you want in a matter of minutes!

As well as the Flight Finger engine, Expedia contains an extremely comprehensive hotel database. Expedia's hotel wizard allows you to set your criteria, such as location, cost, which chain and facilities, and will then find a range of hotels to suit your needs. Many of these hotels contain instant online booking facilities. You simply fill in some basic information, and providing the room you require is available, you will receive an instant booking confirmation. Booking rental cars is just as simple. Here you enter where you would like to pick up and drop off the car, the type of car you require, and any other options such as transmission type and air conditioning. Expedia will then provide you with a range of options, all of which can be booked online. As well as all the DIY options Expedia also provides a limited range of last minute package holidays, although Bargain Holidays does this better.

Another option for the UK traveller is Bob Geldof's DeckChair site (http://www.deckchair.com). This is a refreshingly simplistic website, where the pages don't look cluttered or overcrowded. However, this simplicity does present some problems. It has a lot less in the way of content than sites such as Expedia - but this is fine if you are in a hurry, or don't want to be blinded by vast amounts of options. As with Expedia, it's possible to do a search to find the flight you're looking for. This uses the standard criteria; Airport of Departure, Destination, and so forth. You can also use the online calendar to help you sort out the dates.

If you want a real bargain holiday, then perhaps you should check out the aptly named Bargain Holidays (http://www.bargainholidays.com).

They offer plenty of last minute deals, and the site is always welcoming, with a bright and sunny colour scheme. It is an easy site to get around, and there's plenty of information accessible from the main page including a selection of the best deals currently available. The £99 and under section is particularly interesting. Deals usually include holidays such as a week in Ibiza for £99 or Majorca for £59. To book a holiday found on Bargain Holidays you need to phone their sales team. This is pretty painless, but it would be nice to have online ordering capabilities added to the site. If you like, you can leave an email enquiry which is useful if you want to avoid getting talked into anything on the phone.

The top 20 holiday destinations are listed on the main page, which links to the appropriate destinations currently available. If you fancy getting a real bargain, then you can bid for a holiday using their auction facility, provided in association with QXL (http://www.qxl.com), a European Internet Auction site. It is true that Bargain Holidays do exactly what they say on the tin. Well worth a look.

A2B Travel (http://www.a2btravel.com) offer a very stylish Website, which offers many different services. These include insurance, flights, accommodation, rail and car hire, and weather information (something which is often neglected by other sites). They even go so far as to claim that they are 'Britain's most comprehensive online travel resource - ever'. It certainly seems that anybody wanting to arrange themselves a holiday could probably sort out everything that they need directly from this site, and not very many sites can claim to do the same. There are massive databases of thousands of destinations in the UK and around the world! You can search by town name, so you can first find a flight, and then book yourself into a nearby hotel reasonably painlessly. It's not just accommodation that's featured either, you can also read about the local libraries, art galleries, museums, restaurants, nature parks (the list goes on and on)! You certainly won't be stuck with nothing to do if you have researched your destination with A2B! A lot of time has clearly been spent on this site, making it a 'must visit' if you plan on taking a holiday.

Crystal Holidays (http://www.crystalholidays.co.uk) are a real high street Travel Agents, so they are well equipped to deal with all of your holiday needs. Their Website is very smart and attractive (with a nice swirly background), but you should know that there is very little in terms of useful information here. You can't actually book online, but you can either order a catalogue or fill out a booking form. More for the fleeting Internet user.

Thomas Cook (http://www.thomascook.co.uk) should need no introduction. They are one of the biggest high street travel agents, and one of the few to have a decent Website. Unlike Crystal Holidays, they offer a full online booking service, which accepts your credit card details using a secure server. It's an attractive site, and helpful too. There is a small comical character on each page called Catherine, who acts as your guide, ensuring that you won't get lost or confused. Late deals are available, as well as normal-priced holidays and a handy destination guide.

The most striking thing about this site is the presentation. You always feel that you're in safe hands. If all travel companies were to go to the same effort as Thomas Cook, booking a holiday would be an even better experience.

Another last-minute site is the aptly named LastMinute.com (http://www.lastminute.com). It's a good-looking site, but it has less emphasis on travel than many sites. As well as being able to book holidays, you can also send somebody flowers or chocolates, or even bid in their online auctions. Their travel section is quite good, but not spectacularly informative. LastMinute is more the place you go to see what deals they have and buy travel bargains, rather than researching a place you definately want to go to. However they may just have your ideal holiday on deal! They also have online auctions which allow you to bid for hotel rooms, flights and breaks. It is quite possible that you'll find yourself a real bargain somewhere on the site.

Airlines

The past few years has seen the emergence of the no frills budget airlines. All of these airlines offer no frills, cheap flights to many cities in mainland Europe. Most of them have also embraced the internet in a big way, making it by far the easiest way to book flights. One of the most popular, and well known has to be Easyjet (http://www.easyjet.com).

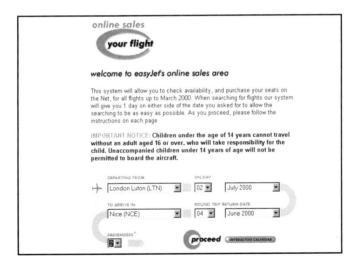

They fly from London and Liverpool to many UK and European destinations. The site provides short cityguides to all the destinations, pricing and timetables, ski information and up to date news. Booking online is a very straightforward procedure and, as an added incentive, Easyjet take £1 off ticket prices for anybody choosing to book on the net.

Ryanair (http://www.ryanair.com) are the Irish airline offering flights between Dublin and twelve UK destinations as well as flights from London, Glasgow and Dublin to many European destinations. They have recently revamped their website and now offer very simple online booking facilities with extra discounts. The site also provides schedules and timetables plus Deals of the Week, some of which are staggering good, to say the least.

Go (http://www.go-fly.com) is the budget airline from British airways. All of their flights go from London Stansted to a range of European destinations. Once again the site has simple online booking facilities and has a range of fare options. The site is also split into business and leisure. Although prices are the same it provides a different angle on destination information and news sections.

Virgin Express (http://www.virgin-express.com) offer cheap flights to a growing number of European cities, usually via Brussels. The website is pretty user friendly and provides selected links to city guide and weather sites. Once again, online booking is a very straightforward affair.

If the budget airlines don't provide the destination you require, or you are looking for more frills then there are still plenty of options open to you. Most major airlines now have good up to date sites with online booking facilities. These can generally be found quite quickly using Excite. If, however, you don't fancy trawling through each company's individual site, there are a few excellent flight booking services. As well as Expedia and Deckchair, which provide their own comprehensive flight search facilities, take a look at Flightbookers (http://www.flightbookers.com) who will find the cheapest flights from many UK airports to virtually anywhere in the world, as well as hotel booking and insurance services. Another good bet is Farebase (http://www.farebase.net). Here you will find a wide range of schedule and charter flights, as well as last minute flights and package holidays.

Other Transport
Many ferry companies now have their own Websites. Some offer the chance to check availability and to book online over a secure site. Others lack these options but do provide other useful information such as the fares and times of crossings. Some ferry companies

even give information relating to their destination country or island. This may include maps and/or details about local food or places of interest.

There are no shortage of companies offering ferry crossings between the United Kingdom and France. SeaFrance, (http://www.seafrance.com) is one such company. Their site includes all the expected information such as the fares and times of crossings. However, unlike many of the other sites, it also features a fairly comprehensive guide to France, which includes practical advice about driving in the country, along with information about French food and places to visit in Northern France. The site also offers you the option to book your tickets online over a secure server.

Brittany Ferries run ferries from the UK to France and Spain. Their Website, (http://www.brittany-ferries.com) is slow and offers only limited information. It does however allow you to request a brochure by completing an online form. This saves you having to visit a travel agent but may mean that you have to wait a while longer before booking your tickets.

If you're looking for a ferry from the UK to France, Spain or Ireland, take a look at the P & O Ferries website, (http://www.poef.com/poef). Details such as the ships' facilities, routes, sailing times and fares are all included. A 'Booking Request' form is also available. This will calculate the cost of your ferry trip, and pass on your booking to P & O staff, who will deal with your request during office hours. The 'Booking Request' form does not allow you to pay for your tickets online but it does provide a convenient service. It is especially useful for those who do not wish to give their credit card details over the internet.

Irish Ferries, 'Ireland's largest shipping company' run ferry services between France, Ireland and the UK. Their site, (http://irishferries.ie) gives details of fares and also allows you to book your tickets online. If however, you would prefer to browse through a brochure, you can request one by filling in a simple online form.

If you're planing a visit to Holland, Northern Ireland or the Republic of Ireland, you might like to visit Stenaline's website (http://www.stenaline.co.uk). On their site you will find timetables, details of fares, a 'brochure request' form and online booking forms. The website is well presented and can even be accessed in six different languages.

If it's speed you're looking for, Hoverspeed, have a Website (http://www.hoverspeed.co.uk). Their fast car ferries run from Dover to Calais and Ostend, from Folkestone to Boulogne and from Newhaven to Dieppe. Their Website is fairly comprehensive and includes company information (including details of the fleet, company history and job opportunities), fares, destinations, shopping (special offers and information relating to products sold on the ferries) and contact information (including a useful 'ask Mike' option). If you have any general queries, you can go to the 'ask Mike' page and type in your question. You should receive a reply within 24 hours. The site also allows you to send a booking form over the Internet and receive confirmation by phone.

If the thought of travelling on a ferry makes you feel seasick, maybe you should consider travelling via the Channel Tunnel. Eurotunnel, 'the operator of the high speed transport system which links the UK to France through the channel tunnel' has a Website (http://www.eurotunnel.co.uk). Information regarding fares and services is available. It is also possible to book your crossing online.

If you want to travel by Eurostar, visit their excellent site (http://www.eurostar.com) for information and online booking.

UK and Ireland travel

The Internet is also very useful for helping you get around inland. For train services take a look at The Train Line (http://www.thetrainline.com) run by Virgin. It provides online booking, seat reservations and timetables for rail travel throughout the UK. Railtrack's site (http://www.railtrack.co.uk) also provides up to date timetables as well as the latest rail news. Most of the UK's rail service providers have their own Websites supplying timetable and fare information. The standard of these sites varies and can normally be found via Excite.

For rail services in Ireland go to Irish Rail (http://www.irishrail.ie). Although there is no online booking facility, you will find news, fares and timetables from Intercity, DART and suburban services.

There are various local bus and coach companies, transporting passengers between different cities within Great Britain. Some of them can be found on the Internet, but few allow you to book your tickets online.

National Express (http://www.nationalexpress.co.uk) are responsible for the UK's major national bus and coach network. They operate services throughout England, Wales and Scotland. Their site is very well constructed. Fill in a simple online form and the cost of your journey will be calculated within seconds. You will then be given the option of booking your tickets online so that they can be sent to you in the post. Coaches travelling to special events are also listed separately along with the cost of travel from various cities. Company information, contact information and links to other travel sites are also provided.

Bus Éireann is Ireland's National bus company. They have Expressway services linking towns and cities in Ireland. Their Website (http://www.buseireann.ie) contains a lot of useful, well-presented information. This includes maps, timetables, frequently asked questions, special offers and links. The only feature it lacks is the option to book your tickets online.

When you decide where you want to go, make sure you shop around. Although all of the online travel agents and booking sites provide much the same service, the prices they charge can vary quite substantialy. The cheapest site for one thing may not be the cheapest overall, so take the time to do the research.

For further sites, see the Travel section in the Website listing section.

11-Shopping

Shopping is either fun or a dreadful bore, depending on your circumstances. If you like walking around shops and spending vast amounts of money on things you never knew you wanted, then the Internet is a necessity. You can buy different things from places all around the world, and you don't even have to leave your home! Paris, New York, London; all of these places have many hundreds of online shops. You don't have to travel any more, just turn on your Dreamcast and shop until you drop.

On the other hand, if, like so many people, you don't like being dragged around shops by your wife/husband/partner or friends, you'll also think the Internet is a Godsend. Sit the offending person down in front of your Dreamcast, with the telephone line connected, and a copy of this book, and get yourself some peace!

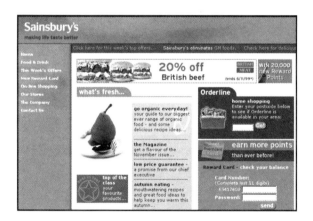

Buying online

Buying online is both easy and safe. It's safe because any decent site will have a Secure Server facility. It will essentially encrypt your personal details (including Credit Card number) before it is sent to the site. Anyone intercepting it won't be able to decrypt it, so you can be sure that it's safe. If a site doesn't explicitly mention that it has a Secure Server facility, you should be wary about sending your details. See if you can phone with them, or even send a cheque. Obviously Credit Card transactions are easier and an awful lot quicker however.

You might think that buying online isn't as good as buying in real life. After all, if you're visiting a real shop you can pick up the item you're buying, and make sure it's in good condition and that it is exactly what you want. Internet shops win major points for being easy to access and massively convenient. You do not have to search far and wide for the best product at the best price and if you order something on Monday, it's quite possible that you'll have it in your hands by Tuesday or Wednesday.

Most of the online shops use a special method to keep track of the things you'd like to buy, known as a Shopping Basket system. It works as you might expect, you simply look around the shop, putting the items you want into a virtual basket. Then, after you have chosen everything you need, you can go to the 'checkout' and pay for your items.

Naturally, it is not just huge chain stores that have an impressive online presence. Smaller shops also have Websites that you can use online, and they are often quicker and more reliable than the big ones. Hobby shops are all over the Internet, so if you have an interest in something such as modelling, stamps or coins, you can be sure to get the best deals online. Smaller shops might not have fancy online ordering systems, and you might have to email the shop owner to reserve an item rather than using a Credit Card.

Online Auctions have really taken off in the past few years. They offer millions of items for sale from all around the world, and you are usually insured against fraud. The end result is that you get a massive selection of items to choose from and a safety-net to fall back on if it all goes wrong. The biggest one in the world is eBay (http://www.ebay.com)

Buying from Abroad

Whether you want to buy something in the US, Canada, Finland or Timbuktu, you need not worry about complications arising from buying abroad.

The first thing you should do if buying from abroad is to check that the shop concerned offers international shipping. Some shortsighted companies refuse to ship outside of their native countries, but thankfully they are in the minority. Most will do it for an extra fee. If it's a large company, you most likely won't be able to bargain with them about the cost of postage - it'll be listed on their site and set in stone! If it's a smaller company however, you might be able to make a deal with them. It always helps if you know how much International postage costs.

The cost for small packages, weighing a couple of pounds (books, videos, CDs etc.) sent from America by Global Priority is around $5 (roughly £3), and it only takes around a week to arrive. If you want the latest, up to date costs, then check out the USPS International Rate Calculator (http://ircalc.usps.gov). Don't let stores get away with trying to charge you £5 to £10 (or even more!), just tell the store (in the politest possible terms!) what kind of postage you would like and how much it costs. Naturally packaging charges may add a small amount on to the price, so make sure that you allow for that.

So, assuming that the company concerned offers shipping to foreign destinations, and that you've sorted out the cost of shipping, you then have to find out a way of paying them. The best way to do this would be to use your Credit Card. This way, the transaction is more or less instant and there's no hanging-around waiting for payment to clear. Also, it costs less, because you don't have to pay to send cash or cheques abroad (which will cost between 50p to £1.50), and also you won't be asked to pay extra money for bank charges (as you might if you sent a cheque). However, there's a chance (especially if you're using ordering from a small business) that the seller may not accept Credit Cards. This being the case, you will have to sort out a cheque (some sellers can accept cheques from English banks, as long as you pay extra for bank charges), and your bank may also be able to provide you with cheques which can be used in foreign banks.

Sending cash isn't usually advisable because it isn't very safe. Compared to cheques, postal orders or credit cards which give you a record of the transaction and offer a from of guarantee, cash offers no such back-up. If you decide to take this route, just go to a bank or travel agent and make your way to the bureau de change. Here you will be able

to get your money changed for around £2.50. International Money orders are also available from banks and building societies, but they cost over £10 each.

Always check with the seller that the kind of payment you are sending is acceptable.

Online Shops

Amazon (http://www.amazon.co.uk) began life in the US, as Amazon.com. They have thousands of books in stock, and can order pretty much any book you like. Their UK Web site now serves English users, but it's always been possible to order from the US branch (if you were willing to pay more for postage, plus taxes). Amazon allows you not only to choose the books you want online, but pay for them online too. They use a secure server to encrypt your credit card information while it is sent to them. For people still sceptical of putting their credit card information online, you have the option of phoning the store with your number. Secure servers really are a safe way of buying things with a credit card however. Amazon claim that nobody has ever suffered credit card fraud after having used their site - and with the level of security provided, this is easy to believe. It's probably safer than giving the information over the phone.

Using Amazon is a simple affair. When you visit the site, you can see a small field into which you type your search words. These can be the names of the author, or the subject of the book you're looking for. When you click 'Go!', you'll be presented with a list of matching titles. You can then pick the ones that interest you. Often they have a further description or scan of the front of the book. If you find a book (or books) that you like, you can just add them to your virtual shopping basket. When you've got everything you need, you have to go to the virtual checkout. Then you just need to fill in some information (address, credit card information), and you're away. You should remember that there are postage costs to pay, but books on Amazon are often quite a lot cheaper than if you bought them in the high street. Price reductions are always stated, so you can make sure you're getting a good deal.

The success of Amazon as a seller of books online has led to a large number of companies offering a very similar service. BOL (http://www.bol.com), Internet Bookshop (http://www.bookshop.co.uk), Bookpages (http://www.bookpages.com), and Alphabet Street (http://www.alphabetstreet.com) are some of the most popular internet only stores.

If you'd rather buy videos, then one of the best choices in the UK is Blackstar (http://www.blackstar.co.uk). They have a massive amount of videos always in stock. You can search the collection online, and every video has its front cover scanned so that you can see what it is you're buying. Each month a different category of videos has 20% off (for example, Science Fiction or Horror). Postage is free world-wide, and they usually ship within a couple of days. They have an absolutely superb range and excellent customer service. Again, they use a secure server to take your credit card details so that they can't be intercepted by malicious hackers.

If you want CDs, rather than something to play them with, then one of the biggest sites in the world is CDNow (http://www.cdnow.com). It is an american site but has loads of amazing features, and just about any CD in the world should be available from there! Based in the UK there is Boxman (http://www.boxman.co.uk). Competitive prices and a simply designed site are backed up with a secure order system.

If you want to order from a name you know then HMV (http://www.hmv.co.uk) is a safe bet. Prices of CD, video and game products are not really any cheaper than in store however.

If you want to buy console games on the Internet then you have access to the official Dreamcast shop directly from Dreamarena homepage. Dreamshop has all the latest Dreamcast games and accessories always available. You can also take a look at the long established Gameplay (http://www.gameplay.co.uk). The price you see is what you pay, so you will not have any additional charge for postage. Delivery is usually within a couple of days. Simply Games (http://www.simplygames.co.uk) is a widely advertised site that also offers very competitive prices for Dreamcast as well as other games.

Jungle (http://www.jungle.com) covers the sales of music, video, DVD and games. The site is lovely to look at and all prices include postage. Goods range from competitively priced to among the best on the internet.

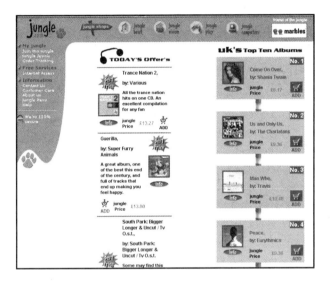

If you want sound and vision hardware then a good site to start with is Unbeatable (http://www.unbeatable.co.uk). They have a wide range of goods, including digital cameras, video cameras and Hi-Fi equipment. For Hi-Fi kit you should also check out Richer Sounds (http://www.richersounds.co.uk). Great bargains are available with online ordering for all your hi-fi and home cinema equipment.

If you want to have your supermarket deliver your groceries to your door then you can right now, if you live in the catchment of participating stores. Tesco (http://www.tesco.co.uk) are adding 5 of their stores a week to their Tesco Direct Internet delivery system. Sainsburys (http://www.sainsburys.co.uk) also have online shopping with deliveries to your door. Again you have to live near a store with the scheme up and running, which is limited presently, but expansion is happening.

If your interests are slightly more diverse, then there's no doubt that the ideal shop for you exists out there somewhere - it's just a case of finding it! You can easily find sites selling anything from ancient coins and artefacts (http://freespace.virgin.net/keith.lloyd) & (http://www.users.globalnet.co.uk/~travis1) to gaming models (http://www.harlequin-miniatures.com). A good place to start if you'd like to find a particular shop is Yahoo! (http://www.yahoo.co.uk). They have very detailed lists of Websites for you to search through, but if you want to do a detailed search then try Altavista (http://www.altavista.com) or Excite (http://www.excite.co.uk).

Buying via Auction

Real life auctions are generally only for the sale of very expensive items, and they can also be extremely daunting for people not used to the auction environment. Internet auctions are a different kettle of fish entirely. For starters, online auctions last for a matter of days, not minutes! They usually last for about a week, which offers plenty of time to get your bids in.

The best and busiest auction site in the world is eBay (http://www.ebay.com). It's based in America, but they also sell items on behalf of people living all around the world. In effect, it doesn't really matter where in the world the item that you are buying is. You can also participate in auctions on Yahoo (http://www.yahoo.com) and Amazon (http://www.amazon.com).

The idea of buying through an auction is one that will put many people off. There are a number of (perceived) pitfalls involved in dealing with individuals on the Internet who may live in entirely different countries. As we described earlier in this chapter, it need not be a painful experience - and ordering goods from abroad is more or less essential if you want to take an active part in online auctions. eBay make it very easy for you to deal with people abroad, and even provide a UK site which provides translation of the prices (usually listed as $US) into UK pounds. Beware that at the time of writing, this feature is extremely bugged and unreliable however, and you are strongly advised to simply stick to the American site - using another site such as the Exchange Rate

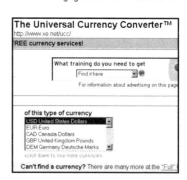

Converter (http://www.xe.net/currency) to convert the prices.

Buying on Ebay (http://www.ebay.com) is fairly straightforward. If you know *exactly* what you're looking for, simply type it into the field and click 'Search'. It will search all of the current auctions to try and find what you're looking for - but take into account that it might be slightly slow, because there are always at least three million items for auction at any given time. With a bit of luck, you'll find what you are looking for on the next page, once your search is completed. If you find something of interest click on it to see the full details. Most items have a photograph with them, so you'll be able to see the condition of them before buying.

The best method to find your way around is to actually look in the proper categories. Naturally you can buy antiques and so forth, as well as videos, coins, toys, collectibles, CDs, computers, software and just about everything else you might want too!

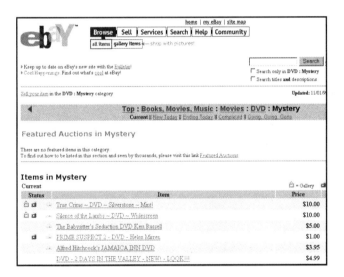

Before you get all excited, you will need to get registered with eBay before you can bid. This is free and very easy. It won't take very long to do, and you'll soon be wondering how you lived without the miracle of eBay! You'll find the registration link on the main page. First you need to enter a bit of personal information, then you will be given your own user ID and password. Keep these safe, because you'll need them if you want to bid for something.

The best thing to do is to keep the pages relating to items you're interested in bookmarked. That way, when you want to see what's currently for sale, it just takes a couple of clicks to get there. Also, it's especially useful to bookmark the 'Ending Today' screen of any interesting categories. This allows you to get all the bargains at the last minute when there is no time for someone to bid above you!

However, there are some circumstances when you'll need to do a 'global' search. This means searching the entire site, instead of just searching in one section. For example, if you wanted a video of Titanic, you could do a search for 'Titanic VHS' from the main page (but beware buying incompatible NTSC videos from the US - unless you have a modern video that can cope with them).

Once you've found something that interests you, then you should check out the box at the top of the screen. It contains information such as the starting price, the number of bids, the time remaining on the auction, and the current highest-bid. The first thing to do is decide how much you're willing to pay for it. It's advisable to enter your maximum bid right from the start. Don't worry, nobody will be able to see what your maximum bid is. eBay works using a special automatic-bidding system. Let's take an example:

> You wish to buy a CD. Its starting price is $2, and there's no reserve price. Imagine you were willing to pay $8 for it - you should enter $8 in your bid amount. Then, when people view the auction they'll simply see that the highest bid is $2. If they then bid $6, the price will go up - but you'll still be the highest bidder, because the eBay bidding system will remember that you were willing to pay up to $8. But if the rival bidder then put in a bid for $9, then the bid would rise to just above your $8 limit. eBay will email you and let you know - you can then chose to bid higher if you think it's worth it.

If it sounds difficult in theory, it's simple in practice.

Dutch Auctions are slightly different. Dutch Auctions are for selling a number of (usually) identical items. So, a seller might have a hundred pens for sale. He offers them up on a Dutch auction for $2 each - that means that you could order one pen for $2, or ten pens for $20. If all of the pens were sold, the price might go up as other people put in higher bids.

If you want to buy something in a Dutch auction, the only real difference is that you'll be asked the quantity required as well as the maximum bid.

A good way to judge the reliability of a seller on eBay is to check their feedback. Feedback is left by buyers and sellers alike, to allow other eBay users to know who they're dealing with. You can check the feedback of someone on eBay by clicking the number next to their username. On eBay, usernames are always displayed with this number beside them, like this: djoser (10). 10 is the feedback rating for that particular user. Click the number to read all of the comments left for that particular individual. If that person has a number of bad comments, you might want to rethink dealing with them - and if they have any whatsoever, make sure you read them.

If you deal with somebody via eBay, it's a good idea to leave feedback for them. You can do this by clicking on that person's feedback rating and clicking the bit that says 'leave feedback'. Then you can leave your own comments. If you're putting negative comments, be sure you've had a good stab at trying to sort your problems out with the seller first. Comments can never be withdrawn.

If you feel somebody has left you unfair feedback, you can respond to it by viewing your own feedback in My eBay.

eBay UK and US has insurance measures in place, in the event of fraud (for amounts up to $200). If you feel you've been defrauded then you're advised to check out the Safeharbor page, (http://pages.ebay.com/services/safeharbor/safeharbor-insurance.html).

Auction tips
If you want to bid for an item, do it in the last 24 hours. You're less likely to be outbid then, and also you'll have a better idea of what sort of price the item is going to raise.

eBay will also host your own auctions for pretty good rates - details are on their site.

Use My eBay (http://pages.ebay.com/services/myebay/myebay.html) to keep track of transactions, your feedback, and your favourite categories.

Always be wary when buying antiques - fakes are occasionally sold. Always check feedback of sellers and check that they know what they're talking about!

If it's not explicitly stated, ask a seller how much they charge for overseas posting before bidding to prevent nasty surprises.

Buying via Newsgroups
Newsgroups are another option. There are vast amounts of items for sale in a huge number of usenet groups (see Newsgroups on page 43). Even if the groups themselves aren't related to the buying and selling of objects, you may find that 'fan' groups will occasionally have appropriate items offered for sale. The main downfall is that you probably won't have any comeback if the seller decides to take your money and run.

12-Lifestyle

The Internet is useful for more than just larking about looking at celebrity pictures and buying the occasional book. It can also change your life.

You want a job? Get one on the Internet. Want some friends? Get some on the Internet. You want a wife? Buy one from an online Russian marriage catalogue. No, but seriously, the Internet can really help you out. It's more than just the odd online job or dating agency, it's an absolutely massive resource with the power to make you rich, popular and successful, if you're willing to make an effort (and if you're a bit lucky).

So how do you harness this power? Well, you've taken the first few steps. You've bought yourself a Dreamcast, you're on the Internet, and you've already learnt how to use email and the Web. All you need to know is where these jobs, friends and cut-price wives are!

Employment

If you need a job, then the Internet is an absolutely invaluable tool. There are more employment sites that you can shake a sizeably-proportioned stick at, and if you send your CV to all of them, you're almost bound to get some interviews. Unfortunately, this does mean that you'll have to re-copy your CV every time you want to send it to a company (the Dreamcast doesn't allow you to save text files yet), but it's worth it considering what you'll get out of it if it works!

Of course, the Internet cannot actually get you the job. It won't help you if you turn up to interviews in a T-shirt and trainers for a future in banking; but the advice you need to make a good impression is all out there somewhere. Take, for example, 'Best Resumes on the Net' site, which contains oodles of advice and tips to get that all-important job. You can find the Website at http://tbrnet.com/.

Resume Tips

General Tips

1. If you have to mail your resume to a prospective employer, do not fold it. Use a large envelope.
2. Spell out everything on your resume. Do not use abbreviations like St. for Street or Ave. for Avenue.
3. Have a friend proofread your resume.
4. DO NOT PUT "References available upon request" on the bottom.
5. When fixing your resume, be sure to use black ink on plain white paper.
6. Use inkjet or laser printing, and avoid dot matrix.
7. Copies of a resume should be clear, and without smudges.
8. Do not use a font larger than 20 point.
9. A graduating college student should keep their resume to one page.
10. If your GPA is a 3.0 or higher, include it.
11. Include any internships you have done within your education section.
12. Do not get too fancy with your resume unless you are applying for an advertising or related position.
13. Most resumes are scanned into computers, so make sure the important points of your resume are on the white section of the paper.
14. Use the 2 digit code for states with no periods in between. RI for Rhode Island etc.
15. Phone numbers should include area codes.

If you just need a helping hand in getting an interview, then a company such as 3D Recruitment (http://www.3dr.co.uk) might be willing to help you out. They will gladly take your CV off your hands, and parade it around in front of potential employers. They deal mainly with Information Systems jobs, however, so they won't be suitable for everyone. Another IT based recruitment agency is Castle Recruitment (http://www.recruit.co.uk), which allows you to apply for jobs online. Obviously that's no good if you'd rather do something like, well, being a dinner lady at a local school. Well, as luck should have it, there's a site out there called Foodjobs (http://www.foodjobs.co.uk). They have plenty of jobs on offer, but won't distribute your CV for you. Still, if you're an unemployed gourmet chef, then it's got to be worth a try.

Most of the big recruitment agencies have an online presence. Reed Recruitment (http://www.reed.co.uk) have a good interactive site. Jobs are divided into relevant sections, and you can expect up to 20,000 of them. You need to register before using the site, but that is a small price for the potential reward.

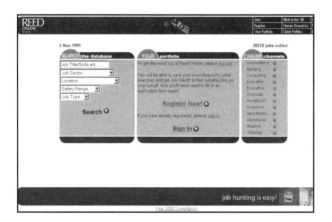

If you prefer taking the fight straight to the employers, you can do that too. Companies such as Asda (http://www.asda.co.uk), Sainsbury's (http://www.sainsburys.co.uk), Cadbury (http://www.cadbury.co.uk) and Tesco (http://www.tesco.co.uk) have special recruitment pages, which you can use to find out about the latest vacancies. They aren't the only ones either. Why not try looking up the Webpages of a company you'd like to work at?

Newsgroups can also be useful. For example, a quick post in uk.jobs.wanted with a brief overview of your experience & qualifications, and a bit about the kind of job you're looking for might prove effective - state in your post that you'll send your CV on to anyone who requests it. If you want to have a look at jobs on offer, you could have a look in uk.jobs.offered. If you just want to discuss your options with a bunch of like-minded jobseekers, you could do a lot worse than uk.jobs or uk.jobs.d (.d meaning discussion).

If you really want to impress, you could set up your CV as a Website (see the guide to creating your own Website, on page 57). If you want to make it really impressive, you'd have to use some graphics (meaning access to a PC or Mac with Internet access), but the Dreamcast could do the bulk of the work. Give it some decent promotion in the proper places (not by spamming Newsgroups) and it might just work.

If you find yourself being turned down due to a lack of qualifications, then why not try an Open University course? It's got to be better than sitting around bored all day. You can find their Website at http://www.open.ac.uk. You can have a browse through their prospectus, or you can get in contact for some more information.

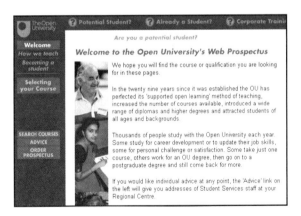

The Internet is a very useful tool if you intend on getting yourself qualified - and if you don't believe me, just do a quick search on Yahoo UK (http://www.yahoo.co.uk) - there are literally hundreds of sites out there, all eager to take your money and train you up to an employable standard.

Dating

There's no shame whatsoever in using a personal pages or dating agencies. Lots of very respectable (and normal) people have used them and found them to be an excellent way of meeting new people - even if you don't get married on your first attempt!

The Internet is full of dating agencies and personal pages, and although many are in the US, there are plenty that support UK users too. The most famous one in the US is Match.com (http://www.match.com). They have a very smart Website and offer a special trial period for anyone who wants to dip their feet into the water! You can also read the testimonials or just skip that to search around the archives, and see if anyone takes your fancy.

Another top US based personals page is American Singles (http://www.americansingles.com). The database of members is however also regionalised into most countries. You will find a fair number of people from the UK on the site. Many also have pictures.

Yahoo offers a reasonably comprehensive list of UK based agencies at http://www.yahoo.co.uk/Regional/Countries/United_Kingdom/Business_and_Economy/Cla ssifieds/Personals/. Amongst the sites on offer are Handidate, a site specifically aimed at disabled men and women, and Lovefinder UK, which promises to help find love, romance and friendship.

Of course, most of these sites will charge you money for access to their full databases - they'd be hard pushed to do it for free. But if you do find yourself hankering for a bit of adventure, you may find it's worth the money.

There are also Newsgroups provided for the purpose of meeting people, and these might be worth a try - but beware the odd people that populate Usenet. God knows there's enough of them. Check out the uk.dating hierarchy if you fancy a quick look. Of course, those common-sense rules when it comes to meeting people (always in a public place, and always running away if you don't like the look of them) still apply.

Food and Drink
An important part of life, Food and Drink. For some more than others, it must be said, but we all have to do it. Some of us enjoy it so much that we set up huge, sprawling Websites in its honour. Recipes, food recommendations, restaurant reviews - the list goes on and on.

First off there is Simply Food (http://www.simplyfood.co.uk), a site which has been produced by the Carlton TV Web-farm, which describes itself as being 'for people who love eating and drinking'. It doesn't let you down either, being a brilliantly designed site which is positively bursting at the seams with food-related tomfoolery. You can check out the latest opinions from annoying TV chef Antony Worrall Thompson, or you can use the excellent 'Restaurant Search' facility. It's absolutely brimming over with good ideas, and a load of money has been spent on setting it up and promoting it. If you like food, don't miss it. Seriously.

The BBC, not to be outdone by their Carlton rivals, have set up an equally delicious site at http://www.bbc.co.uk/foodanddrink/, in which annoying TV chef Antony Worrall Thompson puts forwards some of his fascinating opinions. Of course, that mainstay of Food & Drink, Jilly Goolden, also makes a valued appearance. All of the recipes from the show are now included on the site, and there really is an excellent selection of other bits and bobs for you to rummage through. Definitely one for the cook of the house! Just make sure they don't get over-enthusiastic, and take the overly-large step from pot-noodles to Pak Choi, Ginger And Oyster Sauce.

If you're an ardent supporter of the Vegetarian movement, you can visit Veggieland. It's clearly aimed at the more 'far out' Vegetarians among us, and the design is absolutely horrific, but the good intentions are clearly there. For those who prefer their Websites a little more professional, The Vegetarian Society have compiled a great site which contains loads of Vegetarian information. You can find it at http://www.vegsoc.org.

If you're bored of bangers & mash, you could always try something a little more 'classical', and the Internet can help you out there, too. Fancy making yourself some ancient Roman burgers or spicy bread? Well, go for it - the information is all out there. Try http://www.realm-of-shade.com/sweetlady/cuisine/contents.html for a start. You can be sure that these recipes taste like something that you know you should not be putting in your mouth though.

Beer is well represented online, as well it should be. Included on the Yahoo UK list (http://www.yahoo.co.uk/Regional/Countries/United_Kingdom/Business_and_Economy/Co mpanies/Beverages/Alcohol_and_Spirits/Beer/Breweries_and_Brands/) are well over 40 sites. Amongst the gems are the Carlsberg site (http://www.carlsberg.co.uk/), and the Boddingtons site (http://www.boddingtons.com).

Website Guide

•••

The size and ever changing nature of the World Wide Web makes it an impossible task to compile the perfect guide to sites. The following section is however a broad range of much of the best of what is out there. Most of the sites will also contain links to many other sites with related subject matter making them a good starting point.

In order to bring a sense of structure the sites have been categorised into sections. With sites that cover many possible areas within the headings listed, you may have to hunt about sometimes to track down what you are looking for.

To open any of the sites just bring up the L-menu with the left trigger button or S1 on the keyboard. Now select JUMP and enter the address in the box provided. If you like the site once it is open then you can make it a bookmark (use the Right Menu and select Bookmarks). You will then be able to jump to the site without having to type it out again next visit.

All the sites in this guide have been researched and checked. The nature of the web is such that almost certainly you will find some of them no longer seem to exist or have moved elsewhere. That unfortunately is the way it is with mass fast moving technology. You can however search with a Search Engine for lost sites and often find them in different locations.

Note: With the Internet Filter on you will not be allowed into some of the Websites in this guide. To turn the Filter off see page 18.

Art 94

Astronomy 94

Beer 96

Books 98

Business and Finance 99

Camping and Caravanning . 104

Comedy 105

Comics 107

Computing 107

Dictionaries 109

Dreamcast 109

Ecology 111

Employment 113

Extreme Sports 115

Fashion 117

Films 119

Food and Drink 122

Football 125

Games 127

Government 128

Health and Fitness 129

History 136

Hobbies and Pastimes . . . 137

Kids 139

Language 145

Magazines 146

Music 148

Nature and Pets 152

News 153

Parenting 155

Politics 156

Pop Culture 156

Property 158

Psychic 159

Reference 161

Religion 163

Science 164

Science Fiction 167

Search Engines 168

Shopping 169

Sport 176

Strange 179

Technology 181

Television and Radio 182

Theatre and Performing Arts 186

Transport 188

Travel 189

Weather 196

Weekends and Days Out . . 197

Art

Collage
http://collage.nhil.com/
Browse through with the opportunity of buying over 20,000 works from the Guildhall Library and Art Gallery in London.

The Creative Nude and Photographic Network
http://www.ethoseros.com/cnpn.html
If arty black and white photography of the erotic nature is up your street check out this site. Far from being an excuse for showing lots of female flesh, it is actually very well done and very tasteful.

Glasgow School of Art
http://www.gsa.ac.uk
A beautifully made site with loads of Charles Rennie Mackintosh. Work from recent students is also interesting.

The National Gallery
http://www.nationalgallery.org.uk
Highlights of new and recent exhibitions rather than the full 2000 plus paintings. Also information about the museum all in a clear simple site.

Louvre Museum
http://mistral.culture.fr/louvre/
louvrea.htm
Stunning to look at, this site more than lives up to its appearance. Photographs of some fantastic exhibits, a journey around the museum, current and upcoming special exhibitions and opening hours.

Tate Gallery
http://www.tate.org.uk
Very well made and detailed site featuring the General Collection, the Oppe Collection and New Acquisitions, all online at various resolutions.

The Teletubbies Gallery of Fine Arts
http://www.slacker.clara.net/teletubbies
View peoples lame efforts at drawing Teletubbies. Quite bizzare.

Astronomy

Astro Info *
http://www.astroinfo.ch/index_e.html
"Astronomical information in Cyberspace". Daily updates site with

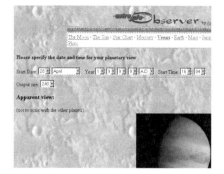

many links to publications. Contains a gallery of pictures of various astronomical bodies/events catalogued by time and location.

The Best of Hubble
http://www.seds.org/hst/
The Hubble had a troubled start to life, but once everything was corrected the results gleaned from it were truly amazing. Check out some of them here.

Galaxies
http://zebu.uoregon.edu/galaxy.html
This archive site offers good quality photographs and images of galaxies, along with links and educational resources.

IAU
http://www.iau.org
The International Astronomical Union. Includes news, events, research, member details and other information.

Mars Pathfinder
http://mars.pgd.hawaii.edu/default1.html

Stunning pictures of the martian landscape are viewable from this site. Along with the Pathfinder's holiday snaps there is also some intelligent discussion of the images portrayed.

NASA Office of Space Science
http://spacescience.nasa.gov/
Check this site out for some stunning photos of the earth as taken by various probes. Information on the technology used to create such images is provided.

NASA
http://www.nasa.gov
The NASA homepage. Includes a huge amount of links to research centres, space flight, galactic anomalies, teaching, technology and astronomy.

The Planetary Society
http://www.planetary.org/
Far from being another paranoid UFO site, this offers intelligent discussion and informative text on the on going quest to find life outside of the Earth.

The Sky at Night

http://www.bbc.co.uk/skyatnight/index.shtml

Very slick site featuring the indomitable Patrick Moore. With news, history, events, glossaries and quiz pages. A must see.

SOHO

http://sohowww.nascom.nasa.gov/index.html

Both NASA and the ESA are responsible for this project which seeks to find out more information about our nearest star, the Sun. Some interesting text and images provide a truly fascinating site.

Welcome to the Planets

http://pds.jpl.nasa.gov/planets

This site centres on our local solar system. With pictures of all of the planets and figures on them to compare and contrast, this is a great place to go planet hopping.

Beer

Bemish

http://www.aardvark.ie/beamish/

Purveyors of genuine Irish stout for over 200 years, this site documents the company's history, including pictures to inspire.

BreWorld *

http://www.breworld.com

European centre for beer and brewing. Fascinating site for both the industry and home brewers alike. It offers information on events, news, organisations, and the perfect ingredients needed for that extra-special pint.

Budweiser

http://www.budweiser.com

Come to the home of the battling reptiles and see the ever popular American lager in all its glory. Find out about the company history, and even get I.D'ed on the way in!

CAMRA *

http://www.camra.org.uk

The Campaign for Real Ale's homepage. Includes links to pubs, tourist information, associated lobby groups, news, and a good beer guide amongst other beer related topics.

famous beverage, as well as games, lifestyle tips, and of course some tongue in cheek toucan based humour. Worth waiting for.

The Good Pub Guide

http://www.goodguides.com/ pubs/search.asp

The online version of The Good Pub Guide detailing pubs in England, Wales and Scotland recommended for their food, drink or accommodation.

Just Brew It

http://www.sgpage.freeserve.co.uk/ index.htm

A good private site dedicated to the Beer Monster, and anyone who loves beer. Good information on home brewing. Book reviews and party tips are also included.

Fosters

http://www.fostersbeer.com

Learn how to throw shrimps on barbies with this bonza website's Australian lessons, then get to grips with the history of the amber nectar.

Fuller Smith and Turner

http://www.fullers.co.uk

Facts about real ales, and information about where to drink them.

Portman Group

http://www.portman-group.org.uk

A site which tries to prevent misuse of alcohol and promote sensible drinking.

Guinness *

http://www.guinness.ie

This site features all the history of this

Young and Co's Brewery

http://www.youngs.co.uk

All the facts you need about Young's real ales. Also details of all the Young's pubs and hotels.

The Virtual Bar

http://www.thevirtualbar.com

Information on all things booze related

including recipes to *induce* the hugest of hangovers and remedies to *reduce* the hugest of hangovers.

Books

Amazon *
http://www.amazon.co.uk
Amazon is touted as the worlds biggest bookshop and can offer you a huge range of titles to buy online. You can use the company's own well developed search-engine to find books and build your own online book store by becoming an Amazon associate.

Bookends *
http://www.bookends.co.uk
Excellent online magazine with news, reviews, links to bookshops, events and authors. Also features guest columnists and storywriters.

The British Library
http://portico.bl.uk
Information about the library's collections and services, along with the document catalogue, current serial databases and connection to the Gabriel network of pan-European library databases.

Computer Books
http://www.compman.co.uk
If you want Dreamcast and general console and PC books then this is a great site that carries most titles in stock for immediate despatch. You can find all the FKB books here!

Discworld
http://www.us.lspace.org
A Terry Pratchett/ Discworld site, containing a wealth of information for fans of the Discworld novels.

Waterstones
http://www.waterstones.co.uk
Good site with news and information on

topical events. You can search the database by a number of criteria for books that are currently in or out of print.

Business and Finance

Abbey National Direct

http://www.abbeynational.co.uk
Need to take some money out but don't know where the nearest machine is? This site will let you know. You can also get in touch with your bank via email.

Alliance and Leicester

http://www.alliance-leicester.com
From the comfort of your own PC this site allows you to apply for a savings account, credit cards and mortgages.

American Express

http://www.americanexpress.com
Whether you're a customer or not, this site could prove of interest. If you haven't got one you can apply for a card. If you have a card you can contact customer services, get a statement and much more.

Barclays Stockbrokers *

http://www.barclays-stockbrokers.co.uk
An online stockbroking service from

Barclays, providing helpful advice and a real time dealing service.

Bloomberg

http://www.bloomberg.com/uk/ukhome.html
This news-oriented site carries all of the main currencies, "hot stocks", FTSE 100 share index information, and links to the other global Bloomberg sites.

Business Wire

http://www.businesswire.com
A convenient way to keep track of how your company is doing. View news as it happens by headlines or full stories, browse through industry specific stories and gather top stories by date or period.

Charles Schwab *

http://www.charlesschwab.com
Daunting to anyone who knows nothing about the subject. It is highly professional, and will really appeal to anyone with a real interest in finance and the money markets.

CyberSpace Law Centre

http://www.cybersquirrel.com/clc/

Lots of things on the Internet are not covered by laws of censorship, copyright and so on, purely because the Web is still so young. This site however has gathered what information there is and presented it in an easy to understand manner.

Calculator

http://www.financenter.com/calcs.html

Although a U.S based site, this invaluable resource offers over 10 categories to build a calculator to work out all of your financial sums and forecasts.

Dow Jones

http://www.dowjones.com

A huge and complete financial news service the lets you tailor the news you receive to your own needs. Plus information on over 10 million companies.

Citibank *

http://www.citibank.co.uk

Using one of the worlds best known banks you can view up to 90 days worth of transactions, view balances, transfer funds, pay and cancel bills and even set up and pay standing orders all online on the site.

Egg *

http://www.egg.co.uk

Providing internet friendly savings accounts, loans and credit cards. Plus the Egg-free zone, which provides independent financial advice and opinions.

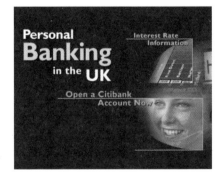

Electronic Share Information *

http://www.esi.co.uk/

If you fancy a bit of share dealing over the Internet, you now know where to come. Also find out how much certain shares are worth and get information on the companies you want to invest in.

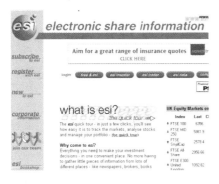

Fidelity UK

http://www.fidelity.co.uk

This redesigned site provides a broad selection of information on investments. Market information is included here as well as interactive tolls and product details.

FinanceWise *

http://www.financewise.com

Containing a bookshop for financial information in addition to comprehensive company data.

Financial Network

http://cnnfn.com

This CNN site enables you to trade 24 hours a day and gives you up to date worldwide financial information.

The Financial Mail on Sunday

http://www.financialmail.co.uk/

This offers more accessible reading of the current financial state of affairs. Easier to use than many others, it is a great site for those with little or no knowledge of the subject matter.

Financial Times

http://www.ft.com/

Although first time users must register to this site, its European news, online prices, articles and interviews are all very worthwhile. There is information on almost all the markets, as well as a "quick view" page, for anyone in a hurry!

Interactive Investor

http://www.iii.co.uk/

Because the Net can be made very current very quickly, news groups have harnessed the technology to bring you extremely current financial reports from all over the world.

Loan Company

http://www.loancorp.co.uk/
If you require a rapid injection of cash, have a look at this site and see if there is anything they can offer you. That car and holiday can be yours!

London Stock Exchange *

http://www.londonstockex.co.uk/
Current figures on the stock exchange can be found here as well as some interesting biography. Learn about our historic financial figurehead and how you can use it. For the beginners there's a dictionary here too.

Lombard

http://www.lombard.com
Lombard offer a direct trading service for everything from stocks to mutual fund investments, subject to membership. This service is backed up by comprehensive online news and free unlimited use of their online quotation service.

Nasdaq *

http://www.nasdaq.com/
No round up of finance related sites would be complete without this firm. Almost everything is offered here, all with sound impartial advice. It is an expansive site to navigate and includes investment tutorials and an online library. A must see.

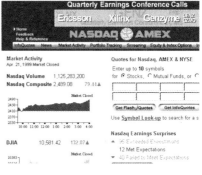

Nationwide *

http://www.nationwide.co.uk
Not only does Nationwide allow you to look after your finances with the click of a mouse. It also provides some excellent links in a very user friendly site.

Natwest
http://www.natwest.co.uk
As well as the standard customer services that are available through this site, there are services and advice sections for doctors, solicitors and more besides. A very user friendly site offering lots of information.

Screentrade
http://www.screentrade.co.uk/
This site claims to be all you need for getting a quote for all kinds of insurance, be it car, home or travel.

Red Herring *
http://www.redherring.com/
Another site devoted to various financial happenings around the world. The usual figures, company reports and backgrounds are available, on a slightly more accessible site.

The Stock Club
http://www.stockclub.com
This uncomplicated site is an extremely useful discussion point for all aspects of stocks and investment. You can choose to enter discussions about your favourite topics and even be notified directly by email if any of your subjects are being discussed.

The Inland Revenue
http://www.inlandrevenue.gov.uk/home.htm
Oh well, it had to happen sooner or later, I knew I should have kept those receipts! On a more serious note, the infamous office are here to help with clear advice and postings on pertinent dates on the tax calendar, along with a tax office database. Don't panic!

Visa
http://www.visa.com
With the Internet now a truly pervasive technology, actual cash changing hands could well be on the slide. Visa wants to be there when it starts to happen. Check this site out for card holder services and promotions.

Wall Street City
http://www.wallstreetcity.com
This site leads you around the inevitable minefield that is investing on the Internet. It lets you know where perhaps the most sound deals are to be had, although nothing of course is guaranteed.

The Wall Street Journal*

http://www.wsj.com/

A good, uncomplicated and extensive site which in addition to all the monetary information gives you advice on how to start up in business. Business travel guides are here too.

The Best of British camping and caravan parks. This invaluable site links the UK's best campsites, with a commitment to quality and reliability of service for its patrons.

Caravan Site finder

http://www.caravan-sitefinder.co.uk/

A well maintained directory site containing lists of regional caravan sites with information to help plan your holiday.

The Caravan Club *

http://www.caravanclub.co.uk/

Official multilingual site available for both members and non-members alike, with comprehensive links and information about the club and its affiliated sites and organisations.

Camping and Caravaning

Best of British *

http://www.bob.org.uk/

Comedy

AAA Jokes Server
http://www.jokeserver.com
Thousands of jokes covering a wide range of subjects. You can join a mailing list to receive a joke a day, and email any that you think are particularly funny to friends. Beware if you are easily offended.

April Fool
http://www.aprilfool.com/
Who needs a reason to play a practical joke? Exactly. Some great online practical jokes to play on friends and enemies alike.

Bert Is Evil
http://www.fortunecity.com/bennyhills/murphy/259/bert.htm/
Fantastic site dedicated to the truth about sesame street's supposed do-gooder. More controversial than watergate, the megalomaniacal dictatorship this once loveable character is trying to create must be stopped at all costs. Scandalous!

Comedy Channel
http://www.aentv.com/home/chcomedy.htm/
This site offers both recorded and live stand up routines from some excellent comedians, from slapstick to alternative.

Daniel Flower Joke Site
http://homepages.ihug.co.nz/~drflower/jokes/
A selection of the most awful and appalling jokes possible. The site splits into general, elephant jokes, mummy mummy and submitted jokes. You can even send in your own to be featured on the site.

Gallery of Advertising Parody
http://www.dnai.com/~sharrow/parody.html
Taking a pot-shot at the advertising industry, the Gallery of Advertising Parody invites you to send in parodies of well known tacky adverts. No company is safe from ridicule.

Humour Database
http://www.humordatabase.com/
An excellent searchable database that will assist you in finding a joke for any occasion by topic, age, or popularity. The cheesy ones are always the best!

105

Monty Python's Flying Circus *

http://www.pythonline.com/

An absolute must have. Some people just don't get it do they? Archive of all the best bits, plus information on what the pythons are up to now. A classic site with cracking illustrations.

Loaded

http://www.uploaded.com/

"Do not enter this site if you are offended, upset or at all annoyed by swearing, coarseness, nudity, or any other fine British traditions." Well-maintained site from the top lad-mag. Up to date stories, jokes, misfortune and of course rudeness are all available here on tap.

Mark's Brush with Greatness

http://www.geocities.com/Hollywood/ Lot/4104/

Quite a humorous site this and packed pull of photos of Mark attempting to rub shoulders with the rich and famous people of the world. George Hamilton,

Leonard Nimoy and Bob Dole all make an appearance.

Men Behaving Badly

http://www.menbehavingbadly.com/

A whole website dedicated to the hit BBC comedy starring Martin Clunes and Neil Morrissey. Learn about the series and the cast. Get to grips with the blokey lingo and join in with a fans forum. Must be viewed whilst drinking lager and dreaming of Kylie!

PAW

http://www.kkcltd.com/paw.html

The Pit of Advertising Wonders celebrates all that is worst about the advertising industry. Enter competitions to create your own spoof headlines and jingles and marvel at other peoples witty or lame duck efforts.

The Stupid Page

http://www.sebourn.com/stupid.html

Dedicated to all things stupid. Read and submit your own stupid stories, jokes and anecdotes.

This Bloke walks into a Bar

http://www.well.com/user/zoodc/bar/ index.html

A database of the Worlds greatest jokes starting with "So, this guy walks into a bar.."

The World's Dumbest Crooks

http://www.dumbcrooks.com/
Specialising in burglars, robbers and all other types of felon who make complete fools of themselves in the line of their illegal duties.

Comics

DC Comics

http://www.dccomics.com
The official site for Superman, Batman, and the rest. You can find the latest news and releases, though ordering is American based.

Garfield

http://www.garfield.com/
Full Garfield site covering comic strips, fan club, fun and puzzles. You can even buy stuff from the online catalogue.

Marvel Comics

http://www.marvel.com
Daily news updates feature in this, the home of Spiderman, X-Men, Marvel Heroes, and the rest of the mob.

Stan Lee*

http://www.stanlee.net
Visit the creator of Spiderman and comic book artist, Stan Lee. Vote for your favourite comic book, and visit the comic book art gallery.

Computing

Apple

http://www.apple.com/
Homepage of the famous Mac. Found here are product updates, help forums, system updates and more besides. The i-Mac and g3 feature prominently, as does online purchasing of products.

Dell

http://www.euro.dell.com/countries/ uk/enu/gen/default.htm
The site of this large supplier of PC's for home and public sector use is well set out, with special offers and technical support. You can make your dream PC here and view the latest kit.

Gateway

http://www.gw2k.co.uk
Gateway's site allows you to review their complete range of PCs and peripherals

and keep up to date with their latest promotions and special offers. They also provide a step by step guide to buying a PC, although there is no on-line ordering facility.

Help Site

http://help-site.com

Providing online manuals and answers to FAQs for all aspects of computing.

IBM *

http://www.ibm.com

A very large site. Here you can keep abreast of the company's corporate dealings, get help and advice online, take a trip around the entirety of this expansive site with their search engine. You can also buy products.

Microsoft UK *

http://www.microsoft.com/uk/default.asp

The Microsoft UK site allows you to view the latest releases and information from the computing giants.

Motorola

http://www.mot.com/

Find out what makes your Mac tick, along with a large percentage of the worlds' appliances and robots. Includes information on all products and sponsored events.

PalmCentral

http://www.palmcentral.com

If you're a Com Palm user then this site has software exclusively for you. Everything is nicely organised and easily searched for.

Tiny Online

http://tinyonline.msn.co.uk

Tiny Online provides not only details of their range of PCs but also has a large amount of general content all powered by MSN.

Dictionaries

A Word A Day
http://www.wordsmith.org/awad/index.html
With the use of this site you will increase your vocabulary immensely. You can even sign up to have a word delivered in your email every day. Soon you'll be baffling your friends in polite conversation and will become a genius on Countdown.

Dictionary of Computing
http://wombat.doc.ic.ac.uk
The Free Online Dictionary of Computing offers its users a fully searchable dictionary of computer terms, links to other reference sites, a random word search and the ability to look up the words closest to the one specified.

Roget's Thesaurus
http://www.thesaurus.com
This site contains an excellent search engine if you are looking for specific synonyms. Alternatively you can browse alphabetically or by "classes" of words.

The Oxford English Dictionary *
http://www.oed.com
The Oxford English Dictionary Online is offering you the chance to help revise one of our greatest traditions. Full history of the publication is on hand, as

is a prototype for the new dictionary.

Wits End?
Http://www.link.cs.cmu.edu/dough/ryhmes-doc.html
The Semantic Rhyming Dictionary offers stumped poets and crossword fans alike an opportunity to find words that rhyme.

Dreamcast

DC-UK
http://www.dc-uk.co.uk/
The site from Future Publishing is specifically designed to run with the Dreamcast console and browser. From here you can chat to other Dreamcast players, take part in polls and discussions, read reviews, and buy games.

DC United
http://www.dc-united.com
A serious looking site supplying, not only all the latest Dreamcast news, but also

training areas and chatrooms.

Dreamcast Europe *

http://www.dreamcast-europe.com

The official Dreamcast website providing news and information of forthcoming events, as well as competitions and an online shop.

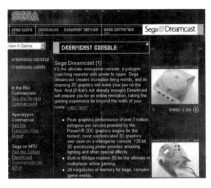

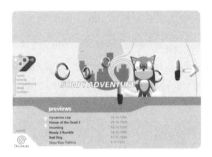

Dreamcast Net

http://www.dreamcast.net

A US site offering news, forums, reviews, previews and cheats for all things Dreamcast.

Official Dreamcast Magazine

http://www.dreamcastmag.co.uk

The site off the Official Dreamcast Magazine. You have to register before using the·site, but it is a painless process.

Sega Dreamcast Net

http://www.segadreamcast.net

News, reviews, previews, screenshots, interviews, codes, contests and more in this up to the minute Dreamcast site.

Sega of America *

http://www.sega.com

Find out about the latest Dreamcast offerings from the other side of the pond with Sega's official US site.

Sega of Japan

http://www.sega.co.jp

The latest Dreamcast news from the country that has it first. Some english language, but far more is in Japanese!

Seganet

http://seganet.com

Part of the Gamefan network. Seganet offers video games news and reviews for all major systems.

Tims Vault

http://www.timsvault.com

One of the webs largest vaults of cheats, providing a complete a-z for Dreamcast. New cheats added regularly.

Ecology

BP Amoco *

http://www.bpamoco.com/

A site that as well as promoting itself, has some interesting statistics and articles on world resources, changes in the climate and related subject matter.

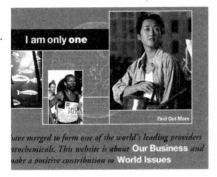

British Trust for Conservation Volunteers

http://btcv.org.uk/

Find out about Britain's largest group of conservation volunteers online. Offer your services, view volunteer and full time vacancies, and shop online to support the organisation.

English Heritage *

http://www.english-heritage.org.uk/

English Heritage's World Wide Web site is a worthy inclusion here, with a conservation section, new archaeology section, places to visit guide and the excellent National Monuments Record.

Friends Of the Earth

http://www.foe.co.uk/

Top site for earthlings who want to make the most of their planet. Tackles issues ranging from genetically modified foods to renewable energy sources.

Greenpeace *

http://www.greenpeace.org/

Well organised, good looking site which focuses on exactly the right areas of the fight for a better ecosystem. Join online, take a tour, or keep abreast of up to the minute developments.

Living Almanac Of Disasters *

http://disasterium.com/

There is a disaster to cover almost any day in the year. Use this site to find out about what disaster happened on your birthday!

The National Trust *

http://www.nationaltrust.org.uk/

Membership, education, history, information, holidays and more are available on this very well presented site concerned with preserving the British Isles.

The Nature Conservancy

http://www.tnc.org/

A good initial guide to the world of nature conservation.

Royal Geographical Society

http://www.rgs.org/

Gather information about the society, its literature and any global issues you feel the need to know about. Still a bit underdeveloped but worth a look nonetheless.

United States Environmental Protection Agency *

http://www.epa.gov/

What is America doing to conserve and improve the environment? Your answers are here, from monetary figures through to the levels of pollution in various places.

Volcanoes.com

http://www.volcanoes.com

This site provides a few facts about the volcanoes of the world, but functions mainly as a stepping-stone to other sites. It also tells you how to go about visiting them.

Wastewatch

http://www.wastewatch.org.uk/
Wastewatch is a site set up to promote recycling. It has practical advice on what to do with your rubbish, provides education packs for schools and a special kids page.

World Wide Fund for Nature*

http://www.panda.org/
This is very good and well-meaning site that enables you to sign petitions against wrong doings the world over. There's plenty here to raise awareness as well as a section devoted to nature artists.

Young People's Trust for the environment

http://www.btinternet.com/~yptenc/
A well informed site offering young people (aged between 5 and 16) the opportunity to get involved with conservation and the environment by joining the organisation, attending field trips and organising school seminars.

Employment

Alec

http://www.alec.co.uk/
Alec's free c.v. and jobhunting page includes links, career advice, and comprehensive interview skills tips.

Brook Street

http://www.brookstreet.co.uk
Top choice for finding full time and temporary positions in the office, secretarial or light industrial areas.

Career Connections

http://www.careerconnections.co.uk/
This site offers career minded people constructive, alternative solutions to both finding work and progressing in their chosen profession.

Give us a Job

http://www.gisajob.com
One of the UK's fastest growing online recruitment agencies.

GTI *

http:/www.gti.co.uk

A useful resource for school leavers and undergraduates who need advice on career choice, information about job availability and training.

Hays IT *

http://www.hays-it.com/

Essentially a site that looks for jobs for you. Give your criteria and hopefully it will be matched. A good looking site too.

Hunterskil Howard

http://www.hunterskil-howard.com/

A large site dedicated to recruitment. This includes lots of jobs from huge

employers NatWest and British Airways. Covering the whole of the UK, there are specialist jobs here too.

Jobsite

http://www.jobsite.co.uk/

A very slick and well presented site. Aimed directly at uniting professional people with jobs and challenging careers across a broad spectrum of businesses.

Jobs Unlimited

http://www.jobsunlimited.co.uk

Nicely laid out site allowing you to search for jobs by sector. There are recruitement consultancy listings and and Inernational jobs section.

Job Net

http://www.netjobs.co.uk

An invaluable site which offers an online database linked to a full compliment of U.K employment agencies and bureaux.

Jobworld *

http://www.jobworld.co.uk/
An excellent job search site which at
first looks messy, but is in fact very user
friendly.

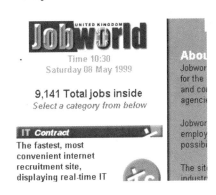

Reed Computing Personnel

http://www.reedcomputing.co.uk/
Huge variety of positions grouped within
areas of the UK. You can narrow down
your search by salary too, which is nice.

Extreme Sports

Adventure Time

http://www.adventuretime.com/
This online extreme sports magazine
covers a good range of sports and
includes reviews of all the new
equipment, and a classified section
where you can buy and sell your old
gear.

ASO

http://www.3rdimension.com/aso/
Good US site devoted to everything
inline. Links to bands, newsgroups and
product reviews as well as skating tips
are all presented in a straightforward no-
nonsense format.

Charged *

http://www.charged.com/
Everything related to extreme sports can
be found here. Backyard wrestling,
climbing, cycling, fun, 'sin', and action
are all covered. A must-see.

Extremists

http://www.awezome.com/
An extreme sports page covering
snowboarding, surfing, motorbikes and
mountain biking. The site includes the
history of each sport, various pictures
and accounts of extreme injuries from
around the world.

Injured?

http://aepo-xdv-www.epo.cdc.gov/
wonder/prevguid/

This essential site offers statistical analysis of the type of injuries involved with (aggressive) inline skating, tips on prevention by the use of protective gear, and help on what to do if you are injured.

Inliners *

http://www.inliners.co.uk/

The U.K's leading inline skate manufacturer. Get up to date on the latest products, safety tips and special offers. Find your local dealer and contact other skaters.

An Introduction to Inline

An icon of our modern lifes the nineties, suitable for all

It's easy to see why people have b and unlike other sports, doesn't re Human propulsion is an environme polluted cities, and a fun way to er

K2 *

http://www.k2skates.com/swfs/fset.html

The official K2 homepage. These guys want perfection in skating, coupled with unique design. This site offers excellent product information, and a good beginners help section along with the usual tips and tricks.

Knowhere Skateboarding

http://www.knowhere.co.uk/skindex.html

Looking for somewhere to do a 360? Have a look at this site for a guide to the best places in the UK to do just that.

Roces

http://www.roces.it/

Aggressive street and course skating at its very best. Find out about the cream of the world's skaters, and also take a look at the great women-only pages.

Tum Yeto Digiverse

http://www.tumyeto.com

If you like to move around on small bits of wood with wheels attached to the bottom, check this site out to have all your skateboarding fantasies come alive.

Xtreme Scene *

http://www.xtremescene.com/

An extreme sports page that covers skateboarding, climbing and snowboarding. View photos, find out about contests and enter real life extreme adventures.

Fashion

Ann Summers *
http://www.annsummers.co.uk/
Book a party, order a catalogue or try out "virtual lingerie" at this risqué site, home of possibly the best girls' night in.

Burton Menswear
http://burtonmenswear.co.uk/

The high street menswear chain can be found online here. Be it smart, casual or sporting this retail giant has it all.

Clothes Care
http://www.clothes-care.com/
"Welcome to your fashion and clothes care guide". If you need advice on fashion or stain removal, or just want to be a part of a million and one soap powder advertising campaigns, then this is the site for you.

Fashion.Net *
http://www.fashion.net
This well-informed site includes a large online shopping section, world fashion links, news, opinions, chat and much more.

FashionUK
http://www.widemedia.com/fashionuk
A site that dedicates itself to all things fashionable. You are even able to ask questions about fashion related things on the site.

FashionMall

http://www.fashionmall.com/

A virtual shopping arcade with fashion shops for the gentleman and the lady. There are also related articles and loads of big names are on offer.

Freemans

http://www.freemans.com/

The catalogue fashion specialist now has online fashion and size guides, as well as the option to buy over the Internet.

Gap

http://www.gap.com

A very plain site but covers clothes for men, women, kids and babies. The clothes are not modelled but simply laid across the page.

Levi's*

http://www.eu.levi.com

A well designed fashion site where you get to look at clothes on real models and rotate the view from different angles. There is also the option play several mini

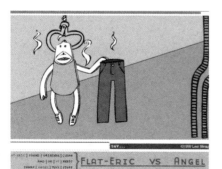

games.

Pepe Jeans

http://www.pepejeans.com

A very stylist jean site, with arty photos of models wearing their products.

SU214 *

http://www.su214.co.uk/

Excellent online menswear store with all the latest fashions and tips on style.

VTRAD

http://www.vtrad.com

Internet Virtual Trading, where you can shop 'till your pad breaks down and your credit card bill goes through the roof! A real gem for the armchair fashion guru if such a thing exists.

Wrangler

http://www.wrangler.com

Wrangler's brand is strongly promoted with the western theme and this site is no exception. Browse the Wrangler catalogue with jeans modelled alongside ten gallon hats. The rest of the range is also represented.

Films

Alfie's Autographs of Hollywood

http://www.alfies.com/

This is a site dedicated to the collection of famous people's autographs and even famous people's addresses. Well worth a look.

Ain't It Cool News *

http://www.aint-it-cool-news.com/

This is a site put together by a film fan called Harry Knowles and apparently a good review by Harry has the potential to affect a film's performance at the box office.

Behind the Scenes

http://library.advanced.org/10015/

This is good interactive site that even allows you to create a short movie online. There's also information on what happens behind the scenes when a film is being made, which is interesting for anyone with a passion for the technical side of filmmaking.

British Film Institute

http://www.bfi.org.uk/

Whether you are just a movie fan or actually learning about the medium itself, there is undoubtedly something here for you. Still very much in development but worth a hit.

Celebrity 100

http://www.celebrity1000.com/main.html

Virtual Oscars and Grammy awards rolled into one. Vote online in a whole host of celebrity polls.

Disney

http://disney.go.com/disneypictures

Site of the latest and forthcoming films from the company that can keep all ages happy for an hour and a half.

Film 100

http://www.film100.com/

Another means of checking out information on films you know and love as well as hopefully discovering some new ones along the way.

Filmsite

http://www.filmsite.org/

Website that lists the 100 greatest films

of all time. Plus another 100 in case they missed any. Also includes sections on Oscar winners and greatest scenes.Also there are the top 100 films from other sources to act as a comparison.

Film Unlimited

http://www.filmunlimited.co.uk

A movie site which covers both cinema and video releases. Contains news, reviews, special features and Hollywood gossip.

Film World

http://www.filmworld.co.uk

Movies site which focuses more on arthouse movies rather than the latest main stream movies. Contains a guide to the year's film festivals, cinema listing and the Videoworld, where you can purchase movies on video and DVD.

The Hollywood Reporter*

http://www.hollywoodreporter.com

A place to keep up on any film related gossip and news. TV programmes and

TODAY'S HIGHLIGHTS

Last Updated By LOS ANGELES / May 7, 1999, 4:28:56 P

FRONT PAGE

'Jones' to pay $25 mil
A jury in Pontiac, Mich., awards $25 million to the family of a man who was murdered after revealing a gay crush during taping of a 1995 episode of "The Jenny Jones Show" that never aired. Lawyers

Film

music are featured here too.

Internet Movie Database *

http://uk.imdb.com/

Search for material on a film, an actor or a director and check out some reviews.

Use The Store, Luke
Got a craving for things Star Wars? Find Star Wars toys, books, mu amazon.com's Star Wars store.

The Final "Stump The Staff"
Next week we'll be unveiling some changes and additions to the IMD exactly what except that it's code-named "The Snack Bar". It's very farewell issue of "Stump The Staff" for more info... (more)

James Bond Home Page

http://www.mgmua.com/bond/index.html

With a half decent actor back in the role of the world's favourite super spy, the Bond movies will be generating a whole new legion of fans. The wealth of information on these Web pages would appear to be more than up to the challenge.

MGM Studios

http://www.mgm.com

A suitably huge Web site for a suitably huge company. The MGM site has information on past releases as well as films that are currently in production. There is also a shop at the site for you to buy some Bugs Bunny ears!

Palace: Classic Films

http://www.moderntimes.com/palace/
A fantastic site dedicated to film noir,
that most atmosheric and charged of all
movie genres. There are many pictures to
download onto your system from classics
such as Big Sleep and Notorious. On top
of this there are lots of well-written
features and articles to keep the curious
happy for hours.

Popcorn *

http://www.popcorn.co.uk
A movie site with reviews, hundreds of
pictures, video trailers and audio
interviews. The Pop Corn site also
contains some cool graphics.

Rough Cut *

http://www.roughcut.com/
US Web magazine reviewing the latest
video releases, behind the scenes reports
and the latest information on
forthcoming hits.

Star Wars

http://www.starwars.com
The official site of the blockbuster
movies. The site is split into four
sections related to each of the four
movies with highly detailed information
on all the characters, spacecraft, planets,
droids, weapons and technology.

The Sync

http://thesync.com/ondemand/
This is a must visit for anyone
considering themselves to be a bit of a
film buff, as well as anyone who wants to
know more about how to broadcast over
the Net.

United International Pictures*

http://www.uip.com/
Have a look at what films are currently
in production from this famous
Hollywood studio.

Universal Pictures

http://www.mca.com/universal_pictures/
A site that allows you to be right up to
speed on movies that aren't even
released in this country yet. That will

impress your friends won't it?

Urban Legends Reference Page
http://www.snopes.com/movies
The Urban Legends Reference Page tells you about all those little snippets of information that people find so interesting. Like the bit in Star Wars where a Storm Trooper bangs his head.

Virgin
http://www.virgin.net/
Possibly one of the best all round UK leisure guides. The site includes a cinema finder and lots of up to the minute entertainment news.

Food and Drink

Buitoni*
http://www.buitoni.co.uk/
Quite a good site concentrating on the

famous pasta sauce. It links recipes with the places in Italy where they originated, and promotes their full range of food.

The Bacon Worship Page
http://www.bqnet.com/bacon
Is your idea of bliss to wake up with the smell of sizzling bacon? If so then visit this site and worship at the altar of pigs.

Ben and Jerry's
http://www.benjerry.com
Company figures and articles on past, present and future ice cream flavours rub shoulders on this site.

Campbell Soup Company
http://www.campbellsoups.com/
Recipes for making whole meals out of a single can of soup and how your body will benefit once you've eaten it. Plus all the details on Campbell's range.

Cadbury
http://www.cadbury.co.uk/
Death by chocolate. The definitive site for lovers of chocolate, old or young. Take a tour of the factory, steal some recipes (!), and play to win more chocolate than you could possibly imagine.

Chateau Online
http://www.chateauonline.com
Indulge in the secrets of France's finest wine. The site includes a gift shop,

recommended wines and a wine search with parameters including name, varietal, appellation and characteristics.

Cookbooks Online

http://www.cook-books.com/reg.htm
An expansive (some say the largest!) collection of recipes all online. From snacks to dinner parties, you will definitely find what you want here.

Cooking Index

http://www.cookingindex.com
For all things culinary. This site provides some mouth-watering treats and great links. Dieters beware.

Creme Egg

http://www.cremeegg.co.uk
Completely devoted to the chocolate egg, this site contains the same wackiness as the adverts and includes egg related mini games.

Food Network

http://www.foodtv.com/
Lots of recipes and lots of advice for the budding chef are provided by this lively and entertaining site.

Foodwatch *

http://www.foodwatch.com.au/
Sound instruction here on how to eat more healthily. Recipes are provided as well as self-assessment tests to deduce how healthily you are eating at the

moment.

Home Farm Foods

http://www.hognet.co.uk/homefarm/
This company offers online ordering of gourmet frozen foods nationwide, with no minimum order or delivery charges and a pay on delivery policy. Delicious.

Hot Lava Java

http://www.hot-lava-java.com/
Every techno-boffin's dream, hot lava java ("the cyber coffee with a high caffeine kick") will keep you awake until the wee small hours. You can play games online, as well as voting for the cup of the month and giving caffeine related feedback.

Ir'n Bru *

http://www.irn-bru.co.uk
"See what Ir'n-Bru can do for you". A really weird site where you can play mad games, view their strange awards, take part in competitions and go orange!

Monsanto
http://www.monsanto.co.uk
Providing the positive argument in the debate about GM foods.

Pillsbury Central*
http://www.pillsbury.com/
This place makes Hagan-Dazs and Green Giant products. As well as recipes there are games and competitions.

The Rare Wine Cellar
http://www.rarewine.co.uk/
Buy wines from a wide variety of years and regions over the Internet!

Real Food
http://www.foe.co.uk/realfood/index.html
Part of the Friends of the Earth site, helping you to "explore the shady world of agribusiness" and track down GM free food.

Recipes For All Tastes
http://www.mwis.net/~recipeman
A massive selection of recipes, along with hints to help you get more out of your kitchen. Visitors to the site are invited to send in their own recipes.

Room Service
http://www.roomservice.co.uk
Only available in London, Roomservice will deliver a meal directly to your door from over 100 restaurants. Simply pick the establishment, select from the online menu and order. Your food will be with you in minutes.

Spice Guide
http://www.spiceguide.com
All you ever need to know about spices. This site covers their origins, purposes, and which go together the best. There are even recipes you can follow to use your new found knowledge.

TuDocs*
http://www.tudocs.com/
This site works as a database for cookery sites on the Net.

TuDocs

The Ultimate Directory Of Cooking Sites

Ah ... the Kitchen. The glue which binds families, the foundation of culture, and source of a near endless variety of dishes which - rich or poor - improve the quality of life.

With the Web comes a proliferation of recipe and cooking sites, a virtual library which holds tens of thousands of recipes from across the globe, most of which may be accessed without cost. Our directory is designed to speed you to the exact recipe or cooking information you want, and to give you an idea of what you might expect from the cooking sites we have reviewed.

TUDOCS GRADING

🐾	Just made it.

The Vegetarian Resource Group

http://www.vrg.org/

No meat from bonkers cows in these recipes, just healthy and nutritious vegetarian grub. There's a newsletter here too.

Virgin Cola Chat *

http://www.virgincola.co.uk/

Join the "gas room" to chat about almost anything, buy concert tickets on the Virgin ticket hotline, vote on the question of the day and win Virgin goodies.

Football

The FIFA Museum Collection

http://www.fifamc.com/

View and even buy some 2000 football related items. Memorabilia, pictures, movies and tours from all over the world are included on this site as well as sporting equipment, toys and much, much more besides.

Football Fantasy League

http://www.fantasyleague.co.uk/

The Internet can be used either for actually participating in a fantasy league or merely for gathering all the current statistics. This site offers both.

Football Mastercard

http://www.footballcard.co.uk

Show the strength of your dedication to your football team by applying for a Mastercard bearing their logo. Not every team has one but most do, and you'll be safe in the knowledge that you are helping their cash flow problems.

Football Now

http://www.football.nationwide.co.uk

Not everyone supports Man Utd or Liverpool. Football Now from Nationwide provides football news from all over the UK, but with the focus on the lower leagues.

From the Terrace

http://www.fromtheterrace.co.uk/

This fans-maintained site is a great way to really get into the grass roots of football, and even contribute material yourself. Check out your local club section.

Global Football

http://www.intermark.com/

Keep up to date on the worldwide football scene with Soccer News Online, no matter who you support this site will prove interesting.

MatchFacts

www.matchfacts.com/

Another excellent virtual football universe, also featuring full coverage of the "real world's" week in football.

Pele, Ole

http://www.math.swt.edu/~ec33032/index.html

A website dedicated to the great man himself. Loads of information on a man whose name should really have been spelt, G-O-D.

Rete!

http://www.tin.it/rete

If you want to stay in touch with the European football scene, log on here for news, fixtures and clips from recent matches.

SoccerNet *

http://www.soccernet.com

Up to the minute information on all English and Scottish leagues, the F.A cup and more.

Teamtalk *

http://www.teamtalk.com

Now fully revamped, Teamtalk provides unrivalled news and information on English and Scottish league teams and the UK's national sides.

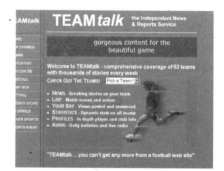

The Football Pages

http://www.ukfootballpages.com

The United Kingdom Football Pages

Directory. Find the team you are looking for in this well stocked no-frills database of U.K clubs. A little stripped down, but containing comprehensive content and a user friendly interface.

Upfront

http://www.upfront-online.co.uk/
Well informed website focusing on the struggle for the acceptance of women's football into the mainstream. Match reports, discussion forums, news, links and feedback make up this comprehensive guide.

Games

The Adrenaline Vault

http://www.adrenalinevault.com
A site for computer game addicts. There's news about the industry as well as the usual wealth of reviews, tips and demos.

Capcom

http://www.capcom.com
The creators of the legendary Street Fighter and Resident Evil series of video games. The site includes links to its Japanese, American and European offices, information on new products, art gallery and an online store where you can purchase exclusive merchandise.

Games Domain*

http://www.gamesdomain.com
Great site this with plenty of information and interaction.

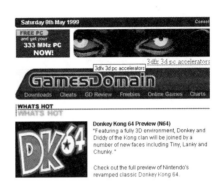

Gamespot *

http://www.gamespot.co.uk/
Very much based around the U.K gaming scene. A very good source of current information that is well presented. You can enter competitions, and view charts and cheats.

Happy Puppy

http://www.happypuppy.com/
Stuck trying to kill that freaky thing in

House of the Dead 2? Be stuck no more with the cheats, hints, tips and solutions that this site offers.

Konami

http://www.konami.com/

The official site for the Japanese video game company responsible for the million seller Metal Gear Solid. Includes product information and exclusive insight to their back catalogue of titles.

Online Gamer *

http://www.ogr.com/

The Online Gaming Realm. This site is absolutely stacked to the brim with news, information, reviews, advice, previews, industry insider information, hardware ratings and more. If you want something games related then they have probably got it.

Pokemon World

http://www.pokemon.com

The website of Nintendo's sensational

craze contains the latest Pokemon news and more than enough plugs for related products.

Total Video Games

http://www.totalvideogames.com

A video game site covering Playstation, Nintendo 64 and Dreamcast systems. Includes news, reviews, previews and an extensive range of cheats, player guides and game translations.

Government

10 Downing Street *

http://www.number-10.gov.uk/

Have a look around the home of the Prime Minister at this eye catching site. Lots of in depth politics as you would expect, but also some history and biography of past PMs.

British Army

http://www.army.mod.uk/

If you've been tempted to join up by the

advertisements on the TV, check this site out for all the information you need.

British Defence Staff

http://www.bdsw.org

This site outlines joint defence initiatives and details of defence relations between the UK and the US. From this site you can examine the British view on policies such as arms control and defence planning.

British Monarchy

http://www.royal.gov.uk

Photos, press releases, and history. For those with an interest in all thing royal this site is fairly basic, but certainly worth investigating. You can find out about the palaces and their visitor information.

Foreign and Commonwealth Office

http://www.fco.gov.uk/

A very informative and current site, providing knowledge in areas such as our relations with other countries and any diplomatic missions that may be underway.

Government Information Service

http://www.open.gov.uk/

Do you want to know exactly what the government is doing for this country as well as others? A huge site containing mountains of information.

HM Treasury

http://www.hm-treasury.gov.uk/

Not the most exciting site, but if you want to keep on eye on the goings on of the Chancellor, look no further.

Local Government Association

http://www.lga.gov.uk/

Providing information on local government issues and details of activities. News and press realeases keep the world abreast of those economic regeneration and sex education in school issues.

Metropolitan Police

http://www.met.police.uk

The site for the greater London police force contains news reports, a page of Britain's most wanted, information on recruitment and an in depth history of Scotland Yard.

Health and Fitness

3 Fat Chicks on a Diet *

http://www.3fatchicks.com/

Good title for this Website and descriptive of the content. Follow the ups and downs of three dieting ladies to see what they are doing right or wrong.

Acupuncture Homepage

http://www.demon.co.uk/acupuncture/index.html

Comprehensive site containing information about the history of the medicine, treatable conditions, research and resources for both patients and practising professionals.

Alcoholics Anonymous

http://www.alcoholics-anonymous.org

Giving information for those addicted to alcohol, with tests to see whether you need their help.

Alternative Medicine Connection

http://www.arxc.com/

An up-to-date site focusing on both the politics and scientific commitment to alternative treatments. Includes an online mail service for patients to exchange help and guidance on what they have found beneficial.

American Heart Association

http://www.justmove.org/

Combat the onset of heart disease by adhering to the advice proffered on this site.

Anxiety

http://www.firststeps.demon.co.uk/

The organisation First Steps To Freedom offers support programmes for those with anxiety disorders.

ASH

http://www.ash.org.uk

As well as being designed to help you give up the dreaded habit, the ASH site also includes helpful advice about suing the tobacco companies of the world and tells you the things the industry does not want you to know.

BeWELL.com *

http://www.bewell.com/

Become and stay both physically and mentally tip top by taking the advice at this site. For men and women.

Bio Rhythms

http://www.facade.com/attraction/biorhythm

Get in tune with the planet earth by creating your own personal biorhythm chart. Change your life or oddball hokum? You decide.

Blood Transfusion

http://www.blooddonor.org.uk

The home of the U.K blood transfusion service, vital to the health of the nation. Sign up today.

Body, Mind and Modem

http://www.bodymindandmodem.com

If you are interested or even just curious about the martial arts of Aikido and Ki, a force that gives us a strong sense of positivity, have a look around this site. The site also contains exercises and advice.

Boots

http://www.boots.co.uk

Beauty tips and health advice from Britain's leading pharmaceuticals retailer.

The British Stammering Association

http://www.stammer.demon.co.uk

The world over, thousands of people suffer from this impediment to their speech. This Website goes about the task of raising people's awareness of this problem.

CMP Media

http://www.netguide.com/health/

Herbal medicine gets a look in here, along with the latest health related news.

Drkoop.com *

http://doctorkoop.net/

An extensive health and fitness site, this allows you to check up on how four people are getting on with their new fitness regime.

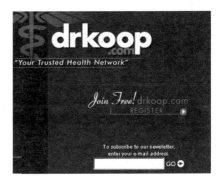

E-sthetics

http://www.phudson.com/

This takes a look at a hospital for plastic surgery, detailing operations that are available along with a few tasteful photographs.

FDA

http://www.fda.gov/

FDA stands for Food and Drug Administration, an organisation who will let you know exactly what's in your drink, your food, and basically anything else you put down your neck.

Fitness Online

http://www.fitnessonline.com/
One of the most complete and
comprehensive fitness related Web sites
around. There are sections where you can
shop for fitness goods and ask questions
as well as features to watch and read.
Very extensive.

FitnessLink

http://www.fitnesslink.com/
As well as providing information on
other health and fitness related sites,
this site has plenty to offer you on its
own.

Go Ask Alice

http://www.goaskalice.columbia.edu
Although this site has a strange name, it
is in fact a very accessible site dealing
with the personal problems encountered
by men and women of all ages. Subjects
covered include alcoholism, drug abuse
and sexual problems.

Health and Fitness Forum

*http://www.worldguide.com/Fitness/
hf.html*
If you want to achieve a full bill of
health this is the site to check out.
Advice on various issues including how
to maintain a healthy diet and sports
medicines are given a down to earth
approach.

Health Education Authority: Trashed*

http://www.trashed.co.uk
An anti drug site that sets out to inform
rather than to preach. Select a drug from
either the drugs listed or via the search
engine. Then learn about its origins, its
effects, how the drug is seen under the
law, the composition, and what you
should do if you discover someone has
taken the drug.

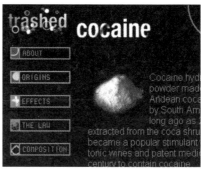

The Health Site

http://www.bbc.co.uk/education/health/
Another good site from the BBC
incorporating detailed sections on health
matters, a quiz that determines your life

span and a listings database. There is also advice for the medical student and the consumer.

Healthfinder
http://www.healthfinder.com/
A good starting point for health related Internet searches. Lots of facts are crammed in.

Hypnotica
http://www.bcx.net/hypnosis/
This site is essentially a guide to hypnotising yourself in order to cure yourself of something or improve an aspect of your life.

IFIC *
http://ificinfo.health.org/
Excellent site of the International Food Information Council. With a wealth of information for both the public and educators drawn from comprehensive resources, this is a must-see.

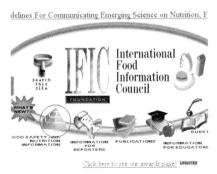

Institute for the Study of Drug Dependence
http://www.isdd.co.uk
A site that takes a more scientific view of drugs. Includes the latest drug related statistics and a library where you can search its database of reports, articles and journals.

Internet Addiction *
http://www.internetaddiction.com
This site takes a light hearted but informative approach to what can be as dangerous to your relationships with friends, family and finances as much as other forms of addiction such as drinking and smoking.

L'Oreal
http://www.loreal.com/
An eye catching site from L'Oreal containing product information and beauty tips.

MedicineNow
http://www.medicinenow.co.uk/

A great site which offers personal, confidential advice and answers on a huge range of medicinal topics. It does involve a small fee, but the professionals involved in the organisation are second to none.

Mediconsult.com

http://www.mediconsult.com/
This is a valuable site offering people with various illnesses the chance to contact someone who can lend a helping hand.

Medisport

http://www.medisport.co.uk/
Using questions to break down the possibilities, this site defines the right procedure and product to aid recovery from injury. There is also a section providing possible preventative measures.

Men's Fitness Online

http://www.mensfitness.com
With so much health and beauty literature around for women it became only a matter of time before men became the subject matter. Take a visit to this site and get rid of those love handles.

Merck Publications

http://www.merck.com/!!ruUsi1bxuruUsk0 nzu/pubs/
Have a look through the Manual of Diagnosis and see if you've got anything

nasty! Much of this site is merely self-promotion, but there is a lot here for medical professionals and curiosity value.

NFSH

http://www.blonz.com
The Blonz Guide to Nutrition, Food Science and Health. Maintained by Ed Blonz PhD this site concentrates on nutritional ways to improve your health. Many links are included, all of which are personally checked by the man himself.

Patient U.K

http://www.patient.co.uk/
Everything you could possibly want as a patient is here. Almost all illnesses are discussed here, and extra features include self-help, ethics and complimentary medicine.

Quit Smoking Company *

http://www.quitsmoking.com
It may work for you, it may not, but whatever you get from this site, at least you can say you tried!

QUIT SMOKING INFO
Quitting Articles/Info
Quit Smoking FAQ
Methods for Quitting
Submit Your Method
In the News
Search This Site

CHAT AND BBS
Bulletin Board System
QuitSmokingChat.com

PRODUCTS
Product FAQ
All Products

Th

Inside, you'll find lots of great information o
ways to make quitting easier, even if you a

We've also got an email newsletter that yo
articles, tips and smokers' stories, plus spe
email box. Just type your address below a

Just Released

Quitting smoking shouldn't be completely s
Check back each Tuesday for another hila

Regaine

http://www.regaine.co.uk

A site for bald men the world over. This Regaine site offers help and advice to the follicley challenged and answers the myth that bald people make better lovers.

Scotland against Drugs

http://www.sad.org.uk

An initiative set up in Scotland to try and prevent children from taking drugs. The site explains its goal and how it intends to tackle the drug problem through educating young people, parents and business.

Summer Skin Care

http://www.icnet.uk/news/sun

This site most importantly informs you how best to prevent skin cancer and also what to check for on your own body. It lets you know who is most at risk and what measures to adopt with regards to your children.

Turnstep.com

http://www.turnstep.com/

Without many illustrations to show how its done, it may be a bit difficult learning some of the 4000 routines listed on the Turnstep site. But with such an extensive selection of routines from all over the world, you should find something to suit you.

U.K Healthcare

http://www.healthcentre.org.uk/

The guide to UK medical information on the web. Includes a clinic with resources for patients and carers, resources and forums for healthcare professionals, site of the week and a useful site search facility.

Viagra

http://www.viagra.com

For the bare facts on a product that has already been hyped beyond belief take a long hard look at this Viagra site. It explains what the drug is all about and also what problems may be caused from its use.

World Health Online

http://www.who.int

The website from the world health organisation provides information about all the latest health issues facing the world today.

Wrecked

http://www.wrecked.co.uk
This site from the Health Education
Authority encourages people to think
sensibly about alcohol.

Yoga

http://www.timages.com/yoga.htm/
A great personalised yoga routine can be
found here. Pictorial representations of
all the required positions are on hand
along with healthy lifestyle tips.

History
....

The Ancient Sites Directory *

http://www.henge.demon.co.uk/
An excellent guide to the UK's
prehistoric monuments. Offers a
searchable text index with links to all
prehistoric sites, with information,
background, and location/travel details.

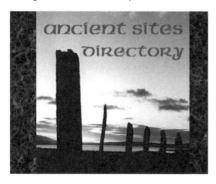

Archaeology Network

http://www.lib.uconn.edu/ArchNet
This University run site offers an
invaluable service by searching a
worldwide library of resources by region,
subject and era. Also has links to the
more famous universities and
organisations.

Egyptian Archaeology

http://www.memst.edu/egypt/main.html
Linked to many examples of mummies
and artefacts. This site includes full
displays from exhibitions and the chance
to take a virtual tour of Egypt.

History of the World *

http://www.hyperhistory.com/
A gigantic online reference
encyclopaedia, which is presented in an
entirely original way. There are important
happenings from all over the world and
features on the people who have made
the world what it is today. Hard to
define but simple to navigate.

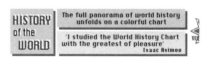

This webpage shows a sample of the original World History
the award winning project HyperHistory Online, accessible wi
better).

HyperHistory Online is based on the synchronoptic conce
regarded as a companion to the World History Chart of Andr
History Chart can be obtained from here. (An enlarged versio
displayed in many Luxury Hotels around the world as a millen
Hyper History is growing monthly until the project provides a

Megaliths

http://www.sonepages.com

The Stone Pages. Full to the brim with information from England, Scotland, Wales, Italy and France. Includes tours, full research backgrounds and other information.

The Natural History Museum *

http://www.nhm.ac.uk/

If you don't fancy a trip to the big smoke to see these exhibits in person, this is of course the next best thing. There's a large library of photographs and some great educational stuff. Hey! Learning is fun!

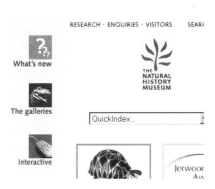

Smithsonian Institution

http://www.si.edu/

An amazingly large collection of artifacts on display at the Smithsonian's Website. This institution has 16 museums in the US, but you needn't leave dear old Blighty to ogle a fascinating site.

Hobbies andPastimes

....

Antiques-UK

http://www.antiques-uk.co.uk

A large online resource for antiques collectors including details of dealers and online catalogues with photographs of over 20,000 antiques for sale.

Birdwatch Online

http://www.birdwatch.co.uk

The homepage of Birdwatch magazine containing features, photos and comments from respected twitchers such as Bill Oddie and Steve Rook.

British Gardening Online

http://www.oxalis.co.uk

This site not only provides plant selectors and lots of links, but also details of gardens you can visit throughout the UK.

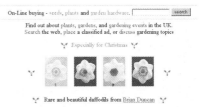

British Horse Society
http://www.bhs.org.uk
Lots of information for the horse lover. The British Horse society's site contains details of riding clubs, diary dates and regularly updated news.

British Walking Federation
http://www.bwf-ivv.org.uk/
This site is packed with information for walks providing, amongst other things, details of trails throughout the UK. If you complete one of their walks you can send off for a cloth badge, how's that for an incentive?

EVENT INFORMATION

EVENTS IN 1999			EVENTS IN 2000		
January	February	March	April	January	February	March	April
May	June	July	August	May	June	July	August
September	October	November	December	September	October	November	December

THE BRITISH WALKING
FEDERATION

BWF EVENTLINE

PERMANENT TRAILS

MILLENNIUM TRAILS

THE AWARD SCHEME

Fishing
http://www.fishing.co.uk/fishing/core/index.html
A UK site containing features and plenty of information for the keen angler. All types of fishing are featured including coarse, game and sea. Very detailed.

Gardeners World
http://www.gardenersworld.beeb.com

A superb site. Gardeners World provides masses of information for gardeners. Including plant of the day, a brief weather forecast, news, tips, events diary, gardeners gallery and even the famous gardeners question time.

Lorryspotting
http://www.lorryspotting.com/index.htm
For spotters of Eddie Stobart lorries (no really!). Containing news and pictures of the large fleet of lady lorries and details of how to join the club.

National Cycle Network
http://www.sustrans.org.uk/f_ncn.htm
The National Cycle network opens in June 2000 and will provide 5000 miles of continuous routes throughout the UK. This site will provide you with all the info.

Ramblers Association
http://www.ramblers.org.uk/
The Ramblers association is at the forefront of campaigns to keep and

maintain public footpaths and give ramblers the right to roam. The site is well laid out with details of trails, events, campaigns, publications and how to join.

Royal Mail Stamps

http://www.royalmail.co.uk/athome/ stamps

The Royal Mails Philatelic services provide details of the latest stamp releases and details of upcoming stamp related events. If ever a site had First Edition written all over it.

Royal Mint

http://www.royalmint.com

A good looking site with all the latest coin related news as well as competitions and coin talk.

Trainspotting

http://www.lexcie.zetnet.co.uk/modular/ mh-trains.htm

Not the cult film with Ewan Macgregor but the real deal. Shunters, locos tube stock and much more, with photos. Ntebooks at the ready then.

Wine Mine

http://www.winemine.com

Plenty of useful tips and information for wine makers to read and share. Something to mull over during the long winter nights.

Kids

• •

Animal Information Database

http://www.seaworld.org/

One of the best nature sites on the Internet, this page is run by the American SeaWorld organisation. Watch feeding and fun with all animals, not just water dwellers. Play games and test your wildlife knowledge.

ArgoSphere

http://www.argosphere.net/

A site to keep the youngsters at bay for a while. Loads of games and quizzes all divided into specific sections. A great resource.

ASfAA

http://www.marlo.com/

The Awesome Site for All Ages. Aged 15-95? Then there's something here for you. Read cartoons, illustrated stories and stockpile some jokes, or simply have fun!

Barney Online

http://www.barneyonline.com/

Probably aimed at slightly younger children, this is an educational as well as fun site packed with animation from the loveable pink dinosaur. Still you don't have to be young to appreciate Barney!

Blue Peter *

http://www.bbc.co.uk/bluepeter/
Remember the glory days of John Noakes and Shep? Explore the archive of presenters old and new and amuse the children for a few hours.

Children' Television Workshop

http://www.ctw.org
Get the lowdown on Oscar the grouch, Big Bird and Elmo with this excellent interactive learning site. All modes of pre-school education are covered very well here, from shapes to memory, numbers to the alphabet.

Colouring In *

http://coloring.com/
A great interactivity site for children, allowing them to choose ready-drawn pictures to colour in, in real-time.

Crayola

http://www.crayola.com/
Some artistic tools for children to enjoy and learn from. There's some games thrown in there too.

CyberPlagrounds

http://www.freenet.hamilton.on.ca/~aa9 37/Profile.html/
This expansive resource features links for children of all ages. Topics covered include science, music, computers, animals, sports, art and more.

Cyberteens

http://www.cyberteens.com/
The aim of this site is to promote creativity and allow kids the world over the opportunity to voice their opinions or ask questions on any topic they like.

The Disney Channel

http://www.disneychannel.co.uk/
A Web site companion to the satellite station. Provides a TV guide to the station as well as information on the presenters.

Disney Online

http://www.disney.co.uk/

Check out clips, cartoons and plenty of animations with the companion site to Disney's satellite channel and EuroDisney.

Dr Seuss' Seussville

http://www.seussville.com/
The Cat in the Hat is back on your laptop! Fun games to play on this site which features all Dr Seuss' brilliant characters. It looks fantastic too.

The Cat in the Hat, Sam-I-Am,Horton and the Whos, and the rest of the Seuss characters welcome you to Seussville. Dr. Seuss's playground in cyberspace. You can play games, chat with the Cat in the Hat, win prizes, find out about new Dr. Seuss books and CD-ROMs, and much, much more! What are you waiting for? Let's play!

Enid Blyton

http://www.blyton.com/
For the younger children this site offers the chance watch cartoons and play with Noddy and his old mate Big Ears.

Fox Kids

http://www.foxkids.com/
The popular children's channel website (and home of Woody Woodpecker). Play games, see what's new and join in the activities of the Fox Kids Club.

Foxy Online

http://www.tumyeto.com/tydu/foxy/foxy.html
If you are teenage and female looking for something to do, check out the site at Foxy Online. There are people to speak to if you need help, and also horoscopes.

Goosebumps

http://place.scholastic.com/goosebumps/index.htm
The huge success of R L Stine's Goosebumps books have resulted in various spin off TV series. This Web site is a companion to both the books and the show and a bit of a biography on the author and creator.

Hello Kitty's Tea Party

http://www.groovygames.com/kitty/
Another educational site, this time for slightly younger kids. Loads of pictures and games with plenty of interaction.

How Stuff Works*

http://www.howstuffworks.com/
Although primarily for children, this site has enough to entertain the adults as

well. How do planes fly? How do fridges keep cold when the back of them is so hot? Answers to all these and more.

I Spy
http://www.geocities.com/~spanoudi/spy
Keep the very young engaged with this very simple version of the guessing game.

The Junction
http://www.the-junction.com
A teenage magazine from those people at Virgin. There's places you can chat to other like minded beings, and you can also listen to music, play games or check out the latest gossip

Kids Publishing
http://www.kidpub.org/kidpub
KidPub is an essential resource for all budding young writers providing a forum for the publication of children's stories from around the globe.

KidsZone *
http://freezone.com

A good site for kids who want to feel grown-up. Comics, games, web page tools and a great chat area.

Kidsurfer
http://www.child.net/forkids.htm
Very comprehensive kids' site giving information on other sites they may well enjoy. There are opinions to give and prizes to win.

Lego
http://www.LEGO.com
Welcome to the world of Lego. Get the net lowdown on all Lego products, including the new Star Wars Lego, plus information on theme parks and forthcoming events. Easy to use and fun for all ages.

Letsfindout.com
http://www.letsfindout.com/
A very nice looking American website which will satisfy the appetite of even the most information hungry youngster.

Little Bo-Peep

http://www.megabrands.com/bopeep/
Tots will love this very popular story and they can click on any word for pronunciation. Be warned, the music at this site is a bit grating!

Mania

http://www.mania.com
Pure multi-media heaven can be experienced at this site, where there is information on games, TV shows, movies and even toys. You can buy the toys online.

Mr Potato Head *

http://www.mrpotatohead.com/
Find out more about everybody's favourite spud. Highlights include the Tater Timeline, games for big and little kids and the chance to see the latest Mr Potato Head toys.

Puffin UK

http://www.puffin.co.uk
A site devoted to the off shoot of

Penguin. Meet the author of the month and check out any related TV and video releases.

Reach Out

http://www.reachout.asn.au/
This site is somewhere for depressed and even suicidal teenagers to go for help. There are many services available here to guide both the teenager and the worried parent.

React

http://www.react.com/
This one is primarily designed for teenagers. Subjects covered include articles on what might be considered an average body weight. Teens can chat to each other as well via e-mail.

Scalextric

http://www.scalextric.co.uk/
The website of one of the coolest toys ever produced. From here you can find your nearest UK stockists, see new products and join the Scalextric club.

Shout Magazine

http://www.dcthomson.co.uk/mags/shout
As you would expect from a teenage girls magazine there are horoscopes, fashion and beauty items and articles about health and fitness.

Stage Hand Puppets

http://fox.nstn.ca/~puppets/
This site offers old fashioned

entertainment on new technology. Kids can indulge in some creative writing and other activities.

Stone Soup

http://www.stonesoup.com/

An Electronic Magazine written and illustrated by children aged 8 to 13. Over ten thousand pieces are received every year, and the emphasis is purely on the creativity of young people.

Stone Soup Sample Issue

Our sample issue includes some of the best stories, poems and book reviews from recent issues

STORIES

Emily Ames: A Fictional Biography — *Allison Imitz*
Will Emily succeed in her attempt to flee slavery?
September/October 1999

The Bishop's Tale — *Daniel Levick*
Is there any way to put a stop to generations of war?
July/August 1999

Pain, Pride, Prejudice — *Anna Wong*
Why are the kids in Rowena's neighborhood so cruel?
March/April 1999

Voice of the Gray Wolf — *Kelly Brdecka*
The wolf pups set out on their first hunting expedition
January/February 1999

Fear and Hope — *Vanessa Matic*
Vanessa writes about a war that touched her family deeply
January/February 1999

Techno Teen Advice

http://www.technoteen.com/advice/

A Web site offering help and advice run by teenagers for teenagers. It is both intelligent and extensive in its subject matter.

Teen Challenge WorldWide Network

http://www.teenchallenge.com/

This site aims to help "the transformation of restored individuals into useful, productive, law-abiding citizens".

Teletubbies

http://www.bbc.co.uk/education/teletubbies/

This is another new site from the BBC and if you're a fan there is everything here you could wish for. It really will keep your tot, (and yourself?), amused for a long time.

Theodore Tug Boat

http://www.cochran.com/theodore/

Theodore Tug Boat is a Canadian cartoon and this is a multimedia version. Great if your child is just learning to read with episodes to entertain along with an interactive story.

Thomas the Tank Engine

http://www.thomasthetankengine.com

A good educational site with a lot of games to play. The site is much more beneficial under adult supervision.

Warner Bros. Online

http://www.warnerbros.com

A very big site as you'd imagine, and one

with a broad range of things to see and do. Movies, cartoons, TV and comics take up the space in this well produced offering.

Web.Kids Adventure

http://www.hoofbeats.com/
A creative site for children. Kids from over 50 countries are asked to help on a series of stories called Alien 5. A merging of creativity that could only be made possible by the Internet.

Yahooligans *

Http://www.yahooligans.com/
The ever-popular search engine in a children-friendly guise. Basically as powerful as the main search engine, it has all "dubious" content removed, and kid-specific site pointers.

Language

AltaVista Translator

http://babelfish.altavista.digital.com/ cgi-bin/translate?
A good simple converter of Spanish, Italian, German and French text into English. Still not one for Glaswegian or Cockney then?

Aussie Slang

http://www.uq.edu.au/~zzlreid/ slang.html/
This site is great fun for lovers of language and daytime television alike. It contains an online Australian-English Phrasebook and slang dictionary cobber!

Esperanto World

http://www.webcom.com/~donh/ esperanto.html/
The most successful 'created' language has many good links and news stories here, as well as help and news groups, and a good introduction to the language as a whole.

H.E.L

http://ebbs.english.vt.edu/hel/hel.html/
The History of the English Language. This site has everything you need to know concerning our language from Norse runes to Middle English right up to modern dialects.

Internet Press

http://gallery.uunet.be/internetpress/diction.htm

Perhaps the best place to start looking for those language related sites. This provides information on other online services such as translators and many different types of dictionaries. No pictures but extremely useful.

Klingon

http://www.kli.org/

The Klingon Language Institute. A must have for any devoted Star Trek fan. Here you can gather information on the language and "culture" of the Klingon people and learn to communicate with other Trekkies.

Merriam-Webster

http://www.m-w.com/

This well established publisher takes its first steps on to the Net with this huge and comprehensive dictionary of words, phrases, abbreviations and, quite literally, a lot more.

Magazines

Cosmopolitan

http://cosmo.women.com.cos

There is lots of information on this site. Features include a rough guide to the Internet, skin care information and regular articles on celebrities.

Empire

http://www.empireonline.co.uk

The site of the movie magazine. Regularly updated with news, reviews and previews of the latest mainstream movies.

FHM

http://www.fhm.co.uk

Website of the UK's most popular lifestyle mag for men. Includes features, jokes, hosts of pretty women and an on-line shop selling books, holidays and clothing. Plus a chance to appear in the mag yourself.

Handbag.com *

http://www.handbag.com

Aimed squarely at female surfers, Handbag is a large site providing features, chat, jobs information, horoscopes, listings, shopping and much more. Everything is well presented, if slightly on the pink side.

Loaded

http://www.uploaded.com/

"Do not enter this site if you are offended, upset or at all annoyed by swearing, coarseness, nudity, or any other fine British traditions." Well maintained site from the top lad-mag. Up to date stories, jokes misfortune and of course rudeness are all available here on tap.

National Geographic *

http://www.nationalgeographic.com/

This magazine site is principally focussed on the USA, but its excellently put together and there's a fine selection of old articles to look at.

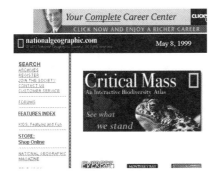

NewsRack

http://www.newsrack.com/

This site narrows down your magazine search by first offering you a globe. Click on a continent, click on a country and then decide what magazine or newspaper you wish to look at. Simple or what?.

Ooze

http://www.ooze.com

Website of rather bizarre magazine which sets out to insult anybody and everybody by parodying popular genre magazines. Not for the easily offended.

Private Eye *

http://www.private-eye.co.uk/

Might not be worth a visit if you subscribe to this magazine, purely because this site echoes it. Still, there's some very witty and sardonic satire here. A great site for browsing through back issues, from 1962 onwards.

Rolling Stone *

http://www.rollingstone.com

Cult music magazine with music news, videos, radio, articles and also take a look at the magazine itself.

Scene One *

http://www.sceneone.co.uk/s1/home

UK entertainment guide, listing all that's happening in the world of cinema, gigs, comedy and live theatre. Plus details of new music, books and video.

Suck Daily

http://www.suck.com

Online magazine taking a quirky look at America and beyond. With a bit of everything thrown in.

Ziff Davis

http://www8.zdnet.com

The site to come to for hundreds of reviews of PCs, peripherals and software. A truely awsome resource if you need some advice.

Music

A&R

http://www.taxi.com

If you want to get ahead in the industry then TAXI could be the resource for you, offering online consultancy from Artists and Recordings people. You have been warned.

Addicted to noise

http://www.addict.com

As its name suggests, this site is devoted to the love of heavy music, namely rock and industrial. News and reviews are available online as well as forums and discussions.

All-Music Guide

http://www.allmusic.com/

A big site with an unflounderable search engine. Read brief accounts of musicians life stories, but more importantly see what records they've released and whether or not they're still available. An American site, but UK bands and performers are in there too.

BowieNet *

http://www.davidbowie.com

Not only a web site containing Bowie related news and music. You also have the opportunity to view his artwork, purchase items from the Bowie store and join his own Bowie Net. All presented in

Bowie's own distinct chaotic style.

BURBS
http:www.burbs.org.uk/
Truly huge site devoted to the profiling
of unsigned British rock bands. Hundreds
of artists feature here, with biogs and
samples of songs available. A must see
site.

Buying Music
http://www.tunes.com/
An excellent online record shop that not
only offers reviews but also allows you to
set up a personal profile and then give
recommendations based on your tastes
in music.

Catatonia
http://www.catatonia.net/
The very sparse website of the slightly
outspoken and very Welsh band. Find out
the latest news and tour information and
buy merchandise online.

Circa
http://www.circa99.freeserve.co.uk/

Minimalist new site from the band being
heralded as the new Radiohead. Find out
what makes the guys tick, the colour and
bands of the month, and send in your
favourite recipes! (and yes.. the drummer
works for FKB Publishing).

Classical
http://www.musdoc.com/classical/
For those with a passion for classical
music they can find everything on this
site from concerts, to new pieces, to
reviews. There is even the option to
enter into discussions.

Classic FM
http://www.classicfm.co.uk/
The Net companion for the magazine and
radio station maintains its aims for
making the world of classical music
approachable for everyone, not just the
select few experts. A good, well
presented site.

Classical Net
http://www.classical.net/
An independent site, but an extremely
good one all the same. Loads of articles
and biographies on the composers and a
guide on how best to begin a classical
music collection. A superb effort.

Dance Music
http://www.juno.co.uk/
This site deals exclusively with
contemporary dance music, be it house,

techno, underground or gabba. Reviews of current and forthcoming tracks are included, along with comprehensive radio and resource links.

Dot Music
http://www.dotmusic.com
A music site which covers news and reviews of the latest pop music. Includes the top 40 UK charts, previews of new songs, interviews and an online shop where you can purchase discounted CDs, albums, singles, vinyl records and music videos.

Drum 'N' Bass Arena *
http://www.breakbeat.co.uk/
An intelligent site aimed at the discerning Drum N Bass enthusiast. Take a trip to the site to read interviews of the genres leading lights, news and also reviews. If your tastes lie with Celine Dion and Genesis, avoid it.

Elevator Music
http://www.midifarm.com/
This page allows you to download a multitude of hits from television, the stage, the charts and more, all in synthesised MIDI format. Bliss.

Elvis Presley *
http://www.mgm.com/elvis/
The MGM site devoted to the king of rock and roll. Visit the Elvis shrine, purchase exclusive gift packages online and even ask a virtual Elvis for advice.

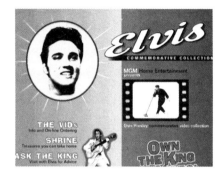

Gramophone
http://www.gramophone.co.uk/
A classical and jazz site from the makers of the magazine of the same name. There's 24,000 reviews from the past 15 years worth of issues along with selected articles and features.

Gigs
http://www.giglist.com/
Keep up to date with all elements of live music in this country with this well-informed gig listing. Find out who's playing where, get up to date on industry news, reviews and ads, and even buy CD's online.

Live Music

http://www.liveconcerts.com/

A great way to catch your favourite bands at their best (live!). This resource offers extensive archiving of live events. Find out where your favourite band has played in the past.

Motown*

http://www.motown.com/

A site devoted to the world's most famous record company. Read about the label's history and learn about classic Motown performances.

MTV Online

http://www.mtv.com/

Aimed entirely at a mainstream American Web audience. Don't expect to be stimulated if you're into the alternative scene in a big way.

Music365

http://www.music365.co.uk/

More mainstream than a lot of sites of this nature, this is a very attractive and current site.

Netaid

http://www.netaid.org/

A website set up to promote development and alleviate extreme poverty across the world. The site was launched with a massive online concert including the likes of Robbie Williams, Bono and the Eurythmics. The site allows you to view star profiles and brief histories of the artists, as well as donate money.

NME

http://www.nme.com/

Love it or hate it, NME has held its place at the top of the British music paper scene for its entire history. Still essential for upcoming tour dates and a good laugh to boot!

Sun Records

http://www.sunrecords.com

The recording company for artists such as Patsy Cline, Roger Miller and The Vogues. Find out more about their artists, purchase albums and clothes online and play sun related games on a slot machine.

The Ultimate Band List *

http://www.ubl.com/

If you've got a cool band name you don't want other bands to nick, register it here. Similarly, check the name you've got doesn't already exist.

different organisations to help protect wildlife and comprehensive lists of extinct animals.

Entomology *

http://www.ent.iastate.edu/imagegallery

A wide range of images and photographs are collated here for insect fanatics. The high quality of the posted shots makes this site a must see for any biologist.

Woodstock

http://www.woodstock69.com

A tribute site to the fabled 60's hippy concert. Contains stories and photos if you need reminding what it was like.

Green cloverworm

Green cloverworm.

Nature and Pets

3D Insects

http://www.ento.vt.edu/~sharov/3d/3dinsect.html

Enter a virtual 3D world of creepy crawlies. Take a look at a wide selection of bugs from a range of different angles. Enough to send shivers down your spine.

Endangered Species

http://www.eelink.net/EndSpp/

Well featured resource site giving information on regions containing endangered species. The site also outlines the work being done by many

Gardenworld

http://www.gardenworld.co.uk/

The ultimate resource for the budding horticulturist. Here you will find a detailed database of garden centres and suppliers across the UK, as well as online shopping, a gardeners diary and garden answers.

The Nature Collection *

http://www.secondnature.com/ nature.htm

Lavish site featuring artwork from many amazing wildlife artists. Montages of images are available to view and add to your screensaver. The wonderfully presented pictures are eye candy of the highest order.

The Pet Place

http://www.ddc.com/petplace

All of your favourite household friends are featured here, including dogs, cats and reptiles. Submit a pets' information for inclusion on the site and read about pet rescue operations and care techniques.

Inter-Species Telepathy

http://www.CyberArk.com/animal/telepath.htm

Spooky site documenting telepathic experiences of pet owners with their beloved animals. Believe it if you will, there are some uncanny instances documented, along with links to other material evidence and discussion groups.

Virtual Cats and Dogs

http://www.virtualkitty.com/

Cool site which allows you to adopt a "virtual" cat or dog, contact other "pet owners", suggest toys and basically have a bit of fun.

News

BBC News 24

http://news.bbc.co.uk/

In most web users eyes, this is 'the' online news site. Clear and unbiased views are well presented, with regular updates and interviews with newsmakers of the moment.

CNN

http://www.cnn.com/

Up to the minute breaking stories form around the globe with America's Atlanta based news giant. From war to cookery, you'll find it here with regular text updates.

Evening Standard *

http://www.thisislondon.co.uk/

The online edition of London's ever-popular rag, the city's top stories are all here as well as the what's on guide, horoscopes and more.

Guardian Unlimited *
http://www.guardian.co.uk/
Most of the news articles that go to making up The Observer and its weekday counterpart The Guardian are available at this extensive site.

Internetnews.com
http://www.internetnews.com/
A site divided into areas including stock prices and business. Also Provides Internet information as well as news.

ITN Online
http://www.itn.co.uk
This ITN news site offers sound news coverage the world over with regular updates amd analysis.

News Index
http://www.newsindex.com

A cool way to find most top international stories. Here you can search a host of publications and online news outlets worldwide.

NewsNow
http://www.newsnow.co.uk
Whether its news on the arts, business matters, sport or whatever, there is a news page here for you.

Omnivore
http://www.way.net/omnivore
Straight-talking news service offering a neutral point of view to the world's top stories as they happen.

Private-Eye
http://www.private-eye.co.uk
Not really news as such, but a refreshing, satirical look at the latest developments in affairs both national and international.

The Chronicle
http://www.thechronicle.demon.co.uk
The UK's first internet news magazine focusing on the affairs of black communities. The site features up to date news as well as community projects and news forums.

The Onion *
http://www.theonion.com
A spoof American newspaper providing funny bogus news stories.

a.v. club

Journalist: Melanie, you've had the last laugh, haven't you'

Melanie Griffith: Huh?

J: You've had the last laugh, haven't you?

MG: What do you mean?

J: People said it wouldn't last—you couldn't do this, you cou and it's lasted and it's going well.

MG: It's still going.

J: Do you feel good about that?

MG: Yeah. But you know what, Jane Fonda said to me when I got nominated for an Academy Award, she said, "Just be prepared. You're going to have many ups and you'll have many downs." I had absolutely no idea what she was talking about, but she was right.

MG: It was like pie to work with Antonio. It was a joy. I think everybody would tell you that.

J: What flavor of pie? Apple pie? Cherry pie? What? How would you characterize it, just for fun?

The Telegraph

http://www.telegarph.co.uk
The Electronic Daily Telegraph offers in-depth home news and top stories with plenty of pictures and background information. Good stop for a daily roundup of top stories.

The Times/ Sunday Times

http://www.the-times.co.uk/ or
http://www.Sunday-times.co.uk/
Save money and paperboy's backs with the times online. Offers the entirety of both papers at the push of a button. Truly a modern publishing breakthrough.

Parenting

Babycare Corner

http://familyinternet.com/babycare/babycare.htm
This site takes a mature approach to answering your Frequently Asked Questions about baby health, growth,

injuries, problems, and behavioural issues.

Babyhood

http://www.babyhood.com
Babyhood's Homepage. This page focuses on infants from birth to roughly 24 months. It includes baby homepages, childcare, health and safety issues, recreation and early reading techniques.

Babyworld

http://www.babyworld.co.uk
Well presented site offering information on all aspects of babies, from pregnancy to feeding. Many related links are available, including toys, competitions, and a baby search engine.

Childrens Express

http://www.ce.org
A news site focussing purely on issues which affect young people.

Ukmums

http://www.ukmums.co.uk
A little lacking in the visual department, this site is still pretty useful for information on all things baby related.

UK Parents

http://www.ukparents.co.uk
A light and airy monthly ezine for UK Mums and UK Dads. Within the site you will find news, features, competitions and forums.

Politics

Internet Watch Foundation
http://www.internetwatch.org.uk
This site is concerned with the publication of all that is illegal and distasteful on the Internet. There are hotline numbers in case you do stumble across something deemed illegal. The page also defines legal and illegal images for you.

Interpol
http://www.interpol.com
Website for the international police. This site provides a reference library and exhibition providing information on Interpol. Includes press release archives and details of the Worlds' most wanted people.

Nato
http://www.nato.int
The site of the North Atlantic Treaty Organisation allows you to get up to date with the latest happenings from their headquarters. The site provides current mission briefings, press releases, and an online library containing archived official documents and publications.

US versus Microsoft
http://www.usvmicrosoft.com
A regularly updated site which counts down the legal action taken by the US Department of Justice against the computer giant Microsoft.

United Nations
http://www.un.org/
The UN's homepage contains detailed information about all aspects of the United Nations work. This includes details of peacekeeping forces, international law, humanitarian affairs, human rights and international and social developments. The site also allows you to review selected documents and maps and read online publications.

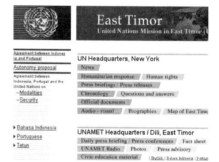

Pop Culture

B*wiched *
http://www.b-witched.com
The official site of the denim clad Irish girlie band. Find out more about the girls, listen to their singles and join the B*witched mailing list.

Who We Are

Boyzone *

http://www.boyzone.co.uk

The official site of Ireland's number one boy band. The site is split into five main categories, The Newz for all the up to the minute gossip, The Boyz where all the members profiles can be found, The Zone for competitions and chat, The Gigz to find out where they are performing and The Tunz for new releases and discography.

Britney Spears

http://www.britneyspears.co.uk

A UK site dedicated to the US Princess of Pop. Site features include a news desk, chat room, picture galleries, song lyrics and a biography.

Buffy the Vampire Slayer *

http://www.buffy.com

The official site of the cult TV hit. Chat with other fans, visit the mortuary to see plotlines of past episodes, play the interactive game and much more.

Eddie Izzard

http://www.izzard.com

The official site of everybody's favourite transvestite comedian.

Emma Bunton Unofficial Fan Club *

http://www.emma-bunton.com

A very good Spicey site containing lots of pictures and detailed information about the Babiest of the Spices. Don't forget to join by sending in your email!

Geri Haliwell

http://www.gerihalliwell.co.uk

Pictures, news, facts and fun stuff. All dedicated to the shy pop star cum UN Ambassador.

Mel C

http://www.come.to/melchome

Regularly updated site containing pictures and news from the sportiest of the Spices, and the rockiest solo singer of the group.

Mel G's World

http://listen.to/I-M-B-W

Inside the site you are confronted with pictures, profile, chat and stories about the scariest of the Spices.

Mr Showbiz

http://mrshowbiz.go.com

A US site providing up to the minute celebrity gossip.

Victoria and David In Love

http://move.to/VictoriaAndDavid

A delightfully romantic site (for those delightfully romanticised by them), containing pictures and news of the UK's most famous pop and soccer couple.

Property

Castle Search:
UK property search agents

http://www.castle-search.co.uk/

Incorporating the whole of the British Isles. Tell this site where you are going and they provide help and assistance. An information and advisory service is also provided via the online magazine.

Find A Property

http://www.findaproperty.com

A site that is always up to date and easy to understand that covers the property minefield that is the south west of London.

GA Property Services

http://www.gaproperty.co.uk

Allows you to search for a selection of properties from GA Property's complete UK database.

Home Hunter

http://www.homehunter.co.uk/
If you're looking to buy a new pad or
looking to sell your old one, you could
do worse than to check here first. This is
a site that deals with the buying and
selling of property all over the UK.

Pro Net – Property Highway

http://www.pro-net.co.uk
This site incorporates all the better
property Web sites and pools them into
one huge database. The information is
broken down into estate agents,
locations, prices and property types. A
good place to start looking for property.

Today's Homeowner

http://www.todayshomeowner.com/
Need some help erecting that fence?
Fancy a makeover of your home? If so,
visit this site and suffer no more in DIY
hell.

UK-Property

http://www.uk-property.com/
An eye catching site where the emphasis
is on finding somewhere quickly to
alleviate some of the tedium of
searching. Includes worldwide as well as
UK properties.

UK Property Gold

http://www.ukpg.co.uk
Placing an advertisement at this site
costs absolutely nothing and is therefore

ideal if you are looking to sell your
home. As well as scoring a huge hit
rating, you can have a picture of your
property online.

UpMyStreet

http://www.upmystreet.com/
Comprehensive is the word that applies
to this great site. Find out about the
suitability and features of any place in
the UK including schools, employment
and house prices. An ideal resource if
you're thinking of moving to a new area.

UPDATE OCTOBER '99
Latest property price data now available.
New: Crime statistics, Primary Schools and Local Council information

Psychic
....

Castle Of Spirits

http://www.castleofspirits.com
Check out some fictional and non-
fictional ghost stories and scare yourself
to death! There are some great stories
here, but feel free to submit your own.

Horoscopes 4U

http://www.horoscopes4u.com
Find out what the future holds in store.
Enter your personal details to receive a
free chart.

Nessie on the Net

http://www.lochness.co.uk
Scotland's first official Nessie web site.
Contains a Loch Ness web camera, so you
can search for the mythical beast from
the comfort of your own home.

Pandora's Box

http://www.pandbox.com
Take a trip to Pandora's Box, a virtual
coffee bar. Read poetry and have your
tarot cards read. Plus more besides.

Reincarnation History

*http://www.best.com/~dna/don/CaseHist
ory.html/*
This well-read site offers actual evidence
of an individual's regression performed
by Don Showen in 1976. Really
believable and spooky, this is a fine
example of the technique.

Russell Grant

http://www.russellgrant.com
The cuddly stargazer provides weekly and
yearly horoscopes and on-line tarot
readings plus quiz games, messageboard
and a biography of the man himself.

Schloss Reichenstein *

http://www.caltim.com/reichenstein/
Find out about Germany's infamous
Baron without a head who lives on the
river Rhine. A guided tour, history of the
castle and even holiday plans are all
here.

Sci-Fi Net

http://www.sci-fi-net.com/
All you sci-fi fans out there can now
obtain your memorabilia on line. Get
hold of videos and books via this site, on
programmes such as The X-Files and Dr.
Who. Break downs on specific episodes
are available too.

SuperScope

http://www.superscope.com
Receive easy to understand online readings
from this slightly simple site.

Tarot

http://www.talisman.net/tarot/
A whole host of tarot card related
information can be accessed here, from

normal readings to specialist sessions, even using an ordinary pack of cards to predict the future.

Uri Geller's Psychic City

http://www.urigeller.com/

Uri Geller invites you to visit his site and see if you have the potential to become a true psychic force. Check out his interesting life story as well and judge for yourself the results of experiments he has undergone.

Witchcraft

http://www.rci.rutgers.edu/~jup/witches

With Joan's Witch Directory you can explore witchcraft throughout the ages. Based around the C15th witch hunting manual, the 'Malleus Malificarum', historically correct information and artwork can be viewed.

Reference

Acronyms

http://www.ucc.ie/info/net/acronyms/ acro.html/

Make sure that your all important logo doesn't already exist in business by searching this site's 12,000+ incarnations of abbreviations.

Alt.Culture

http://www.altculture.com/

This popular resource contains a comprehensive searchable a to z of 90's popular culture. Get the news on films, art and music.

Calculators

http://www.calculator.com/

Calculate everything. By using over six thousand tools you can work out the time you will spend sleeping throughout your life to how much food you need depending on your weight in this constantly-updated resource.

Dictionary.com

http://www.dictionary.com/

A site providing the ability to find the language related information you require. Links to huge online dictionaries are here, including the Oxford English.

Encyclopedia.com *

http://www.encyclopedia.com/

Brief articles but fast searches are the name of the game here, at a site containing a massive free Encyclopaedia.

Encyclopaedia Britannica *

http://www.eb.com/

The Encyclopaedia Britannica Online. Although only available as a free trial for a seven day period, the idea of an online, constantly updated reference set is virtually irresistible!

English/Cockney Rhyming Slang Dictionary

http://www.bio.nrc.ca/cockney/

Cockney rhyming slang is great, and if you can master it you can baffle and amuse your friends simultaneously. Be warned though. There is no standing on ceremony at this site.

Free Online Dictionary of Computing

http://wombat.doc.ic.ac.uk/foldoc/index.html

If you look at a word like 'bitmap' and have no idea what it means, get online and surf the Web for an answer!

Glossary Of Poetic Terms

http://shoga.wwa.com/~rgs/glossary.html

A back to basics approach for this informative site. Very useful for checking pronunciation before you get to class and embarrass yourself.

Information Please

http://www.infoplease.com/

The powerful search engine located at the Information Please site will find almost anything that you want found. Sport, arts, history, politics – nothing major is neglected.

Multi Media Mapping *

http://uk.multimap.com/

Great detailed maps on any place within England, Scotland and Wales, using a point and click format. Type in a postcode or area name and this will take you straight there. Metaphorically speaking of course.

CLICK THE CORRECT SPOT AND WIN $20!

2

Multi Media Mapping

A complete interactive atlas of Great Britain on the Web!!

Just click on the UK outline map to start browsing. Or enter the name o (London only) or postcode to get a detailed map. You can then zoom in area you wish to see in more detail, or you can choose to look at a new the map, you can zoom in and out as you please.

NB: We don't yet have coverage of Northern Ireland - sorry, we're wor

Just click on the UK outline, or enter a place name in the form below an

National Lottery *

http://www.lottery.co.uk

Camelots national lottery site allows you to view previous results, examine number frequencies, and, just for fun, generate six random numbers.

Main Draw Results | Thunderball Results
Lottery Books | Lottery Links | Lottery Software | Lottery News
Historical Results | Statistics | Six Random Numbers | Fantasy Lottery
contact us

Phrase Finder

http://www.shu.ac.uk/web-admin/ phrases/

Provide the site with a word and it will discover phrases connected with that word from a selection of over 5000. Then find out where it originated and what it means. Fantastic!

Population

http://www.sunsite.unc.edu/lunarbin/ worldpop/

This somewhat scary site gives an up to the minute estimate of the world's population. Information on curbing the figure is less forthcoming however.

Quoteland

http://www.quoteland.com/

An excellent site for you to find a quote to suit your needs, whether for an essay or just to prove someone wrong. The search facility will also find quotations relating to specific subject matter.

Symbols

http://www.symbols.com/

No, not the artist formerly known as Prince, but an incredibly useful online resource with the correct meanings for countless historical, chemical and otherwise bizarre signs.

ZDNet Webopaedia

http://www.zdwebopaedia.com/

Not a flashy site by any means but useful nonetheless. Technological language is seemingly forever in fluctuation. Keep up to speed at this site.

Religion

Bible Gateway *

http://www.calvin.edu/cgi-bin/bible/

This comprehensive bible resource is searchable by passage or text reference, which also allows direct linking to its database via the use of hyperlinks.

The Bible Gateway(TM) is a service of The Gospel Communications Network , a ministry of Gospel Films, Inc

BIBLE GATEWAY
A Service of the Gospel Communications Network

Other Languages:
GERMAN
SWEDISH
LATIN
FRENCH
SPANISH
PORTUGUESE
ITALIAN
TAGALOG
NORWEGIAN

More Information:
ABOUT THE GATEWAY

Version: NIV

Passage:

Search word(s):

Restrict search: (assumes whole Bible)

If your search turns up more than 10 verses, t
the results will be shown as references only.

CIN

http://www.cin.org/

Everything related to Roman Catholicism can be found here, from history and papal teachings, right through to recent encyclicals and visits.

Ethical Issues

http://www.acusd.edu/ethics/

A great site for both teachers and students. Many current ethical debates are discussed here, with a relatively unbiased approach.

Global Hinduism

http://www.hindunet.org/

The Global Hindu Network. Teachings, history, culture, philosophy and more are available in this popular religious site.

Insight

http://world.std.com/~metta/

This site focuses mainly on helping practising Buddhists in their meditation technique, understanding teachings and their applications.

Jewishnet

http://www.jewishnet.org.uk/

Jewishnet is the website of Europe's largest online Jewish community. The site provides news, services, shopping and even an online agony Aunt.

Maven

http://www.maven.co.il/

An excellent site with a capable search engine for Jewish or Israeli related links.

Orthodox Christianity *

http://www.ocf.org/OrthodoxPage/

Very well maintained for followers of the orthodox tradition, or simply those who wish to find out about the faith.

Mistras, Greece

Welcome to The Orthodox Christian Page!

Just what is an "Orthodox Christian" anyway?

Click here for a text-only version of the page.

The Orthodox Page   The Orthodox Page

The Vatican

http://www.vatican.va

Stroll around the Vatican's museums, examine the religious statues and artwork and visit the Vatican's own press office.

Science

Annals of Improbable Research

http://www.improb.com/

Most scientists exist to improve and further human existence. Some just explode stuff and do weird things. Some of the latter are here.

Aurora Borealis

http://www.uit.no/npt/homepage-npt.en.html/

A fully featured, factual site which focuses directly on the study of the phenomenon by a Norwegian team of scientists. A clear and detailed explanation of the beautiful lights is available online- Not to be missed.

Earthquakes Online

http://www.civeng.carleton.ca/cgi-bin/quakes/

Information is provided here on all major earthquakes worldwide, along with Richter scale details, damage reports and danger hot-spots.

Encyclopedia of Psychology

http://www.psychology.org/

Students of psychology will find this an invaluable site when looking for definitions of specialised terms.

European Space Agency

http://www.esrin.esa.it

Basically the less wealthy European version of NASA, the ESA, despite its problems, has had some hands on experience with some very successful space related missions. Have a look at their history and discover their plans for the future.

Frank Potter's Science Gems

http://www-sci.lib.uci.edu/SEP/SEP.html

An entertaining site for either the student or the browser. Physical sciences are the focus here.

Horizon

http://www.bbc.co.uk/horizon

Designed to function as a partner to the excellent TV science series, there are items here from past programmes that tread a truly eclectic path.

IEE

http://www.iee.org.uk/

The Institute of Electrical Engineers site offers information on joining the society, along with a calendar of events, a searchable information database and impressive links to other sites.

The International Space Station

http://station.nasa.gov

Although not quite the same as the space station in 2001, the International Space Station is a reality. A very exciting prospect for anyone wishing to spend long days in the big black.

The Lab *
http://www.abc.net.au/science/
A fascinating site dedicated to the study of all the sciences, with question and answer forums, detailed articles and a wealth of information and links.

NASA
http://www.nasa.gov
An extremely busy site this one, especially if something big is underway. A great site with information on everything from the Hubble to the Space Shuttle.

The National Museum of Science and Industry*

http://www.nmsi.ac.uk
A well crafted Website with some beautiful collections and fine text. Oh, and a rotating polygon.

New Scientist
http://www.newscientist.co.uk
The Website of the magazine, which has an immense range of interesting articles on a variety of subjects such as earthquakes and cloning.

Nostradamus Society of America
http://www.nostradamususa.com
Some of what is predicted is right, some is wrong. Still, it's not the end of the world.

Nuclear Power Station
http://www.ida.liu.se/~her/npp/ demo.html
Why not try your hand at peaceful nuclear fusion with this interactive nuclear powerplant.

Popular Science
http://www.popsci.com/
Good quality information delivered in an accessible way from the Website of the American magazine.

Rockets Online
http://www.rocketryonline.com/
Almost tongue-in-cheek site giving details on building rockets for science or pleasure, from back garden specials right

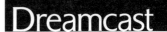
up to fully-fledged missiles.

Science A Go Go *
http://www.scienceagogo.com/
A very simple and well designed site providing all sorts of news and information from the world of science in a very user friendly manner.

Science Daily
http://www.sciencedaily.com/
A constantly updated site with news of scientists who are advancing in their work.

Tomorrow's World
http://www.bbc.co.uk/tw/
In addition to covering the articles on the TV programme this site allows you to delve into the features of past shows.

The X-Prize
http://www.xprize.org
Essentially a competition with a 10 million dollar award, the X-Prize goes out to the first person or group of people to create a working space craft that can be

used time and time again, with a long term goal of providing tourist trips to space.

Science Fiction

Alberta UFO Study Group
http://www.planet.eon.net/~kijek/
The Alberta UFO Study Group have set up this official page designed to investigate and corroborate stories of UFO sightings in Canada, where some 3 million people are supposed to have seen a UFO.

Alien Bob
http://www.pnn.com/~boba/alien1.htm/
Almost every single 'alien' interaction with earth is documented here. Alien species, crop circles, government conspiracies and more are all covered in minute detail.

Aliens are Abducting our Pants
http://www.sock-monkey.com/pants.html
There are a lot of things the people of this world are blissfully unaware of. The fact that aliens are stealing our pants from under our very bottoms is one of them. Lock up your pants!

The Black-Ops Encyclopaedia
http://www.cruzio.com/~blackops

A must for all you conspiracy theorists out there. Although this is essentially still being put together there are some very interesting theories here relating to the Royal Family, Zionism, Presidents and much more.

E.T

http://ebe.allwebco.com/
The Extraterrestrial Biological Entity Page. An absolute wealth of information for believers in ufo's and sceptics alike. Containing documented sightings, news reports, chat groups, links and an E.T. search engine.

ExoScience UFO

http://www.aufora.org/
Not just specifically UFO related stories, this site has news from NASA and science pages.

Paraweb

http://theparaweb.com/
Although there are masses of similar sites around, this online one is a cut above the standard.

X-Files *

http://www.thex-files.com/
The official homepage of the smash television series. Biographies of characters, episode rundowns, a fans forum and links are all included for fans of the show. Possibly a paranormal phenomenon itself! But remember, it's only swamp gas.

Search Engines

AltaVista

http://www.altavista.com/
One of the most powerful search engines on the Internet, you can search web pages and newsgroups using a single word, and also include multiple language searches.

Ask Jeeves

http://www.askjeeves.com/
A great place to start if you don't know where to start! This intuitive engine may seem basic at first but the unusual use of actual questions to probe the Internet can often resault in satisfying information.

Excite *

http://www.excite.com/

This heavyweight of the search engine world offers not only a straightforward search using text entries but also the opportunity to examine its many 'channels where similar sites are grouped together.

Personalize Your Page!
FREE Excite Mail Account
Make Excite My Start Page

Today on Excite

Monday, May 3, 9:38PM EDT
News: Gun Arrest in Littleton
xPoll: Kosovo Breakthrough?
• Hot Jobs Across the U.S.
• Excite Love-O-Meter

Infoseek

http://www.infoseek.com/
Similar to Excite, this search facility offers excellent world wide web search facilities, as well as channels and a customisable format option.

Lycos

http://www.lycos.com/
Lycos provides a great service when you are looking for a very specific topic, with its title-only or URL-only search facilities.

Scoot

www.scoot.co.uk
A local directory giving details of hundreds of businesses in any part of the UK. Very easy to use.

Yahoo! *

http://www.yahoo.com/
When you have time to really trawl the net, Yahoo! is the engine to use. Its fully featured comprehensive directory searches are second to none. One for your bookmarks.

Shopping

Alphabet Street

http://www.alphabetstreet.infront.co.uk
Another in the growing line of online stores selling books, music, games and DVD.

Amazon Bookstores

http://www.amazon.co.uk
Choose from 1000s of books online. Read reviews and get recommendations. Pay by secure credit card or by phone if you prefer.

169

Animail *

http://www.animail.co.uk

An online pet shop where you can purchase a large range of pet related merchandise, including limited edition fine art prints.

Antiques

http://www.londonmall.co.uk/antiques/

Buy and sell furniture, paintings, clocks, china, copper, glassware, gold, silver and more with John Charles Antiques' online services.

The Apple Store

http://www.apple.com/ukstore

This Apple Store site allows you to buy your entire Apple Computer related electronica from the comfort of your own home. Self – explanatory.

Archie McPhee

http://www.mcphee.com/

Buy some quirky gifts for people you know. A voodoo doll. A punching nun. Or even a rubber chicken. Guaranteed hilarity will result.

Audiostreet

http://www.audiostreet.com/

For mainstream rock and pop CDs at discounted prices, in a well laid out site, take a trip down Audiostreet.

Black Star

http://www.blackstar.co.uk/

A massive video store enabling you to search for any title online, as well as search by genre.

Bookpages

http://www.bookpages.co.uk/

Look for a book via the search engine or through a related topic, Bookpages offers a massive range of books on a huge number of topics. A very user-friendly site and one of the most comprehensive bookshops around.

Boxman

http://www.boxman.co.uk

Online CD shopping specialist featuring everything from country to techno. Very straightforward.

B&Q

http://www.diy.co.uk/

You can do it with the help of B&Q's excellent site. Get help for all kinds of home or garden projects, find your nearest store and browse through hundreds of hardware products. All the fun of a Sunday without leaving the house.

British Magazines Direct
http://www.britishmagazines.com/
Specialist and mainstream magazines get a look in at this site. Navigate yourself easily around, find a magazine you want and it should be with you in 48 hours.

Bunka
http://www.bunka.co.uk
An online retailer dealing solely in Dreamcast hardware, games and peripherals.

CD Now
http://www.cdnow.com/
Huge American Web site that sells all music related products from CDs to T-shirts. It can be cheaper to buy from here, despite the postage, than from a UK retailer. Massive array of genres and artists included, and good fun just to browse around.

Conran
http://www.conran.co.uk/
An extensive collection of shops that share a common goal, customer satisfaction through customer satisfaction. Excellent product, and competitive pricing. Most products are claimed to be hand picked by Terence Conran Himself!

Cyber Pet
http://www.icatmall.com/cyberpet
An online pet shop which uses a search

engine to find products rather than directing you to groups of products. This prevents the site from being as instantly accessible as Animail and The Pet Gift Shops sites.

Dixons
http://www.dixons.com
Website of Britains leading electrical retailer. Find out the goings on within the company, check out what's new or locate your nearest Dixons store.

DVD World
http://www.dvdworld.co.uk/
A large selection of DVD titles as well as latest news, a search engine and the opportunity to receive weekly mailouts..

Exchange and Mart
http://www.exchangeandmart.co.uk
Buy or sell anything on-line with the classified ads magazine that has become something of a British institution.

Flowers Direct
http://www.flowersdirect.co.uk/

If you left for work in a bit of a huff this morning, return to a home of warmth and happiness by sending some flowers to your loved one!

Fortnum and Mason

http://www.fortnumandmason.com/
Have a look around a virtual Fortnum and Mason store and if you're not leaving the house for a while, buy a hamper.

Free Classifieds *

http://www.freeclassifieds.co.uk
Submit and review classified ads for a wide range of products and services. Pick up anything from a C-Reg Metro with no MOT, to a blonde, 24-year-old Taurean with GSOH, likes walking and fine art.

Gameplay

http://www.gameplay.com
One of the UK's most well known and trusted games mail order companies. Gameplay offers news, reviews and, of course, the option to buy the latest video games.

GB Posters

http://www.gbposters.co.uk
Hide your wallpaper with a huge selection of posters. That's the idea with this site. Music, film, and television personalities are waiting to adorn your wall.

Giftstore UK

http://www.giftstore.co.uk
A slightly eclectic range of gifts are available at Giftstore UK. As well as cards and flowers, there are also toys, games and equipment for juggling. You will no longer be stuck for gift ideas.

Goldfish Shopping Guides

http://www.goldfish.com/html/guide/mainset.htm
Goldfish have teamed up with a range of companies to offer discounts to their cardholders. Find out more here.

Heffers

http://www.heffers.co.uk/
One of the oldest bookshops around. Heffers embraces the Internet with an excellent site enabling you to order books on an immense range of subjects.

HMV

http://www.hmv.co.uk/
HMV is one of the UK's leading high street record, video and video game retailers. Their website gives you up to

date news, information and special offer details with the option to purchase on-line.

Innovations

http://www.innovations.co.uk
Accompanying the catalogue of the same name that falls out of the Sunday papers. Some of the ideas included here are scarecrows, garden swing seats and electric potato peelers.

Interflora *

http://www.interflora.com
Order flowers online for the one you love. With online help and advice and pictures of the flowers to send no-one need be without happiness.

Jungle

http://www.jungle.com
A mail order site selling movies, music, games and computers. The site offers special offers on a wide range of products and loyalty points to keep you coming back.

The Kite Shop

http://www.kiteshop.co.uk
Some of these kites are very expensive, suggesting that kiting need not necessarily be a child's past time anymore. Some of these kites are amazing structures. This site is a must for the serious kite enthusiast.

Loot

http://www.loot.com
The online service for second-hand bargains. Place ads and view last weeks advertisements for free, or pay a £1.30 fee to browse the up to the minute bargains.

Macys

http://www.macys.com
Browse around the massive on-line Macys department store. Unfortunately UK customers can't order on-line

My Simon

http://www.mysimon.com/index.anml
Decide what you want to buy and My Simon will scour the web for the best deals.

NBA Store

http://store.nba.com
Thanks to its highly paid, highly visible stars, Basketball looks set to build upon its reputation as a happening sport over here. This site provides you with the gear you need to look like and play like a pro.

Nutra Source

http://www.nutrasource.com

The place to come if your feeling run-down, want to stay feeling tip-top, or just can't stand the taste of fruit. Buy vitamins, cod liver capsules or even Brain Boost in huge bulk and get huge discounts from this American company.

Off The Record

http://www.otrvinyl.com

An online music shop which specialises in rare and collectible vinyl records. Items can be searched either by a keyword or by genre.

Office of Fair Trading

http://www.oft.gov.uk/

The Office of Fair Trading site offers consumer help with all sorts of trading standards issues. Plus a special section containing tips and advice for shopping on the internet.

Pet Gift Shop

http://www.petgiftshop.com

An online pet shop that sells a range of products including books, music, games, animal related jewellery and pet accessories.

Petsmart

http://www.petsmart.com

Not only does the Petsmart site sell its range of products but also includes guides for taking care of your pets and the opportunity to adopt an animal.

Plastercast Skulls

http://www.twoguysfossils.com/reprod3.htm

Buy reproductions of fossils and even human skulls. The perfect gift shipped to anywhere in the world.

Pricecheck

http://www.pricecheck.co.uk

Cross-reference prices for utilities, cars, mortgages, personal investment and more with this useful online database.

QXL

http://www.qxl.com

Online auction room where you can bid for anything including art, cars, holidays, CDs, games, videos and books.

Richer Sounds

http://www.richersounds.com/

The online store of the highly regarded bargain hi-fi dealer.

Sainsburys

http://www.sainsburys.co.uk
Shop from home. Check your Rewards balance, get recipes and even play a game of Sergios Crazy Kitchen.

ShopGuide

http://www.shopguide.co.uk
Essential stop for people who want to purchase goods online. This organisation reviews and rates online shopping sites in the UK.

Shopmate

http://www.shopmate.co.uk
Providing links to all the major Internet shopping sites. Decide what type of product you are interested in and Shopmate will supply a brief review of the best online shops available.

Shopper's Universe

http://shoppersuniverse.com
Possibly the best and most complete shopping experience on the Web. Thousands of DIY, games, and sport equipment products are available through this site. Extensive and easy to use.

Shopping Zone

http://shopping.lineone.net
A huge virtual shopping arcade incorporating a huge selection of virtual shops. Everything from music shops through to lingerie shops are featured and rated here, as well as a guide to how

secure the online buying is.

Shops On The Net

http://www.sotn.co.uk
Search for a shop on the Web by shop name, topic, address or Website. The site includes details of special offers and lets you know of any new shops starting up, as well as giving its views on current ones.

ShopGuide *

http://www.shopguide.co.uk/
Take all the hard labour out of shopping. ShopGuide provides links taking you directly to the type of shop you need. Plus an excellent bargain finder facility which trawls the net to find you the best deal on whatever you are looking for.

Simply Games

http://www.simplygames.com
A very well presented mail order site providing news and reviews as well as the latest console and PC games at very low prices.

Tesco

http://www.tesco.co.uk

The website of the UK's largest supermarket. Contains much more than bread and cheese. Book tickets and holidays on-line, check how many clubcard points you've earned and get free internet access. People living in certain areas can go virtual shopping then have their groceries delivered to their door.

Ticketmaster UK

http://www.ticketmaster.co.uk

Take a trip to the Ticketmaster site to reserve tickets for most upcoming shows or concerts.

Toys R Us *

http://www.toysrus.co.uk

Read the online catalogue, check out the latest promotions and offers and buy toys online.

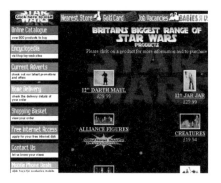

UK Music, Games and Video Store

http://www.musicandvideo.co.uk

Buy music games and videos on-line. Search for particular titles, artists, songs, directors or actors from a range of over 230,000 items.

Unbeatable

http://www.unbeatable.co.uk

A brilliantly designed site allowing you to buy all that is electronic via the Web. Fantastic offers on brand name items are standard with this site, as are the exceptionally detailed specifications.

Sport

All England Lawn Tennis and Croquet Club

http://www.wimbledon.com

Best visited when the championships are in session but still interesting to find out about the history of the place, plus past results and ticket availability and prices.

Autosport

http://www.autosport.com/nav/index.cfm

The website from the bible of the motor racing world. The site provides all the latest news from all aspects of motorsport including Formula One, Rallying and Indycar.

Blue SQ

http://www.bluesq.com

Online betting shop allowing a wager on all of the usual sports fixtures and events plus much more. Here you can also bet on a wide range of subjects such as stock markets, soap opera plots and which member of the Corrs will marry first.

Boxing.com

http://www.boxing.com

When a fight is on, live coverage is available. This is a must for the boxing fan to visit, purely because of the depth of information it provides.

British Touring Car Championship

http://www.btcc.co.uk

Find out where the next meet is, who will be competing, as well as additional information on the teams and drivers.

Bushido Online

http://www.bushido.ch

A brilliant site to look at as the world of martial arts is split open here for all to see.

CarlingNet *

http://www.carlingnet.com

Visit the CarlingNet site for team updates, results, league information and stats.

CricInfo *

http://www.cricket.org

Cricket info covers everything concerning this most British of pastimes. Results, match analysis and news from home and abroad make up this well featured site.

Cricket Unlimited

http://www.cricketunlimited.co.uk/

Concentrating largely on the news aspect this cricket devoted site is kept well up-to-date and details other sites that should be of interest.

Formula1.com

http://www.formula1.com/

Not the official Formula 1 site, but a good effort anyway. Terrific photos to look at and very well written stories on the current season.

Golf.com

http://www.golf.com/

A lavish site devoted to all things golfing. The world-wide news is very comprehensive with all the major pro tours are covered, along with rules, equipment and tips to improve your game.

Grand Prix Legends

http://www.grandprixlegends.com

Here you can order Formula 1 merchandise, which apparently is a bit of a blooming industry at the moment. Model cars, helmets, prints, videos and other official goods are available at this site .

Racing Post Online

http://www.racingpost.co.uk/newsite

Get the latest racing news, view the runners and riders and see which horses the tipsters fancy.

Rugby *

http://www.scrum.com

Concerned with every aspect of rugby. Find global match results, celebrity viewpoints, find out about women's rugby and even visit the bar!

Rugby Football Union

http://www.rfu.com

An official site packed full of information on the history of rugby, rules, upcoming fixtures as well as results.

Rugby League

http://www.rleague.com/

All the latest info is available here, from match statistics to discussion groups, this is believably self titled as the "most comprehensive Rugby League site".

Sporting Life *

http://www.sporting-life.com/

Great resource for fans of all sorts of sports- cricket, racing, snooker, golf, F1, rugby and football are just a few of the national pastimes covered with good depth and accuracy. You can even bet or take part in an online sports quiz!

Wheelbase

http://www.lboro.ac.uk/research/paad/wheelpower/home.htm

The site of the British Wheelchair Sports Foundation providing details of events and competitions. The site also gives contact numbers and addresses for any wheelchair user wishing to take up one of the many featured sports.

Strange

Addicted to stuff

http://www.addicted2stuff.com

A site that asks people to share what it is they are obsessed with. This could be anything from a hatred of poodles to people who mispronounce the word cat. A very funny site, well worth a visit.

The only tools one needs in life:

WD-40 to make things go and duct tape to make them stop.

cars
sports
pick-up lines
bad classified
ads
good words
bad words
quotations
grooming
food/food/food
naming things
venting &
ranting

Hello, Stuff faithful! Welcome to the next evolution of Addicted to Stuff. We have changed a little since the last time you saw us. We have a couple of new categories and a few that we archived. Check out our new Addicted to Sports, Pick-up Lines and Bad Classified Ads!

Cars: From Bronco's to Love Bugs, we love them when they start up, we curse them when

Aliens Ate My Balls

http://artemis.centrum.is/~loftur/ufo.html

A considerably odd site containing a short comic strip about ball eating aliens.

Ask Satan

http://members.aol.com/asksatan/index2.html

A very funny and original site which shows the attempts made by Satan to get some publicity. Great music and hilarious photos of the Devil rubbing shoulders with celebrities.

Casper The Talking Cat

http://www.ibmpcug.co.uk/~artapart/casper

From the Institute of Feline Linguistics comes Casper the talking cat. Although not a huge conversationalist, what utterances he does make are suitably earth shattering.

Conspire *

http://www.conspire.com

Is OJ Simpson part of the Japanese mafia? Is Bill Clinton a serial killer? Are people having brain implants as a part of secret government experiments? Probably not!

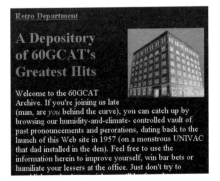

Retro Department

A Depository of 60GCAT's Greatest Hits

Welcome to the 60GCAT Archive. If you're joining us late (man, are *you* behind the curve), you can catch up by browsing our humidity-and-climate- controlled vault of past pronouncements and perorations, dating back to the launch of this Web site in 1957 (on a monstrous UNIVAC that dad installed in the den). Feel free to use the information herein to improve yourself, win bar bets or humiliate your lessers at the office. Just don't try to

Fortean Times

http://www.forteantimes.com/
The Website of the magazine dealing in strange paranoia. The site contains breaking news stories, an archive of articles and much more spooky stuff besides.

Kooks Museum

http://www.teleport.com/~dkossy
People who have been described as kooky include Bjork and David Icke. This site is devoted to kookiness in all shapes and sizes. There's a kook museum, a hall of hate, a hall of quackery and loads more strange stuff.

ET Corn Gods

http://www.etcorngods.com
Discover hidden subtext within the English language with this site from the ET Corn Gods. Learn how to use their language to bring forth strange stuff.

Guide to Ultimate Reality

http://www.rishi.dk/guide/
Why do things exist? If this is a question to which you have long searched for an answer, have a look here and see if everything suddenly becomes clearer.

Human Radiation Experiments

http://tis-nt.eh.doe.gov/ohre
Provides information on what the title suggests, most of which occurred during the cold war.

The Naked Dancing Llama

http://www.frolic.org
Take philosophical advice from a Naked Dancing Llama whilst watching him shake his funky thang!

Subliminal Messages In Windows 95

*http://www.tcp.ca/gsb/PC/
Win95-subliminals.html*
This is a mad site which claims that Windows 95 incorporates subliminal messages and images including a picture of Jimi Hendrix being all romantic with a horse.

The Tackiest Place In America Contest

*http://www.thepoint.net/~usul/text/
tacky.html*
If you ever get the chance to drive across America, take it. For on your journey you may come across a 30-foot lobster. Here is a site dedicated to interstate insanity.

The T.W.I.N.K.I.E.S Radiation Test

*http://www.twinkiesproject.com/
radiation.html*

There are a lot of sites devoted to the art of blowing up food. This one is no different as it attempts to blow up a twinkie in a microwave. Science has come a long way.

Viking Remote Viewing
http://www.viking-z.org/
Viking remote viewing, psychic self defence, UFOs and crop circles. Read at your own risk.

Voluntary Human Extinction Movement
http://www.vhemt.org/
A site that tackles the problems connected with the over population of the world by us humans. Sensible solutions are offered in an entertaining way.

Technology

B&W
http://www.bwspeakers.com
At prices ranging from £100 to £35,000, B&W have speakers for everybody and every price bracket, whether you're a paperboy or Richard Branson. Plus a good glossary of terms.

Binatone
http://www.binatone.com/
Sometimes remembered for a somewhat 'budget' feel, the Swiss company's website is anything but that. It boasts music and an excellent online catalogue, which speaks volumes for their sales and marketing departments.

Braun
http://www.braun.de/
Good site dedicated to the German manufacturer of electric toothbrushes and coffee perculators. A very well presented site with good product information proving you can have brains as well as Braun.

Denon
http://www.denon.co.jp
The best of all the Oriental hi-fi makers, Denon have put together this site which allows you to have a look at their equipment, including their new style retro machines, plus lists of stockists.

Hi-Fi Playground
http://www.hi-fi.com
The place to go for up to date news on the ever changing world of Hi-Fi.

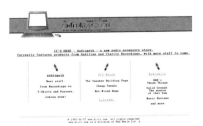

PLEASE NOTE : All information on this web site is relevant only to the UK

Hotpoint *

http://www.hotpoint.co.uk

Very cute animated site with full product line specifications, history, hints and tips and a spares help section. The company also invite you to contact them regarding a wide range of corporate feedback schemes.

Kenwood

http://www.kenwood-electronics.co.uk/

Take studio quality hi-fi and put it in your car! That's the main point behind this excellent site from Kenwood. There's a section here where you can tailor the best system for your needs.

Linn

http://www.linn.co.uk

For the absolute finest in hi fidelity, check out the Web site from this British manufacturer, Linn. Browse around the vast selections of equipment on offer and then decide if you can afford one.

Philips

http://www.philips.com/

Expansive site from the European consumer giant. Addresses both corporate and home users with a new technologies section that is well worth a look.

Television and Radio

Adbusters

http://www.adbusters.org/

This is a great site for anyone who has ever felt conned and lied to by either a TV or Magazine advertisement. It is a nicely put together swipe at the products themselves as well as the people trying to sell them.

The Adam and Joe Show

http://www.channel4.com/entertainment/adam_and_joe2/

Adam and Joe's off-the wall humour is broadcast on Channel 4. These teddy bear loving surrealist pranksters will be looking to expand their already large fanbase.

Babylon 5 - Docking Procedures

http://www.babylon5.com

This site can be used by fans who want to discuss and share their opinions on what's great and what grates about this sci-fi series. The usual cast information and clips are available too.

Baywatch

http://www.baywatchtv.com

If you want behind the scenes gossip on past and present stars of this shiny, happy programme, check out this site and be transported into the sun along with loads of pretty women and hunky men.

BBC Online

http://www.bbc.co.uk

Want a career at the Beeb? There's a vacancies section here, along with all the things the BBC is famous for such as news, weather and education.

Beeb

http://www.beeb.com

Where the BBCs other sites take themselves just a little too seriously, this one is a breath of fresh air. There's a Comedy Zone, a section for Top Gear and something called the Score, where you

can get the latest information on all that is sporty.

Brookside

http://www.brookie.com

Get up to date with the plot, view the family trees, buy Brookie products, and take a backstage tour at the official Brookside website. Calm down.

Capital FM

http://www.capitalfm.com/

Shows what will be broadcast and when, special pages allotted to the DJs, plus news and weather.

Carlton

http://www.carlton.co.uk/

Not just TV listings at this Carlton site, but also sections dedicated to issues raised in the programmes it transmits.

Channel Four

http://www.channel4.co.uk/

A brilliantly designed site, as you might expect from Channel 4. It has information on all the programmes it currently puts out which is put across in a lively, fun and sometimes slightly off kilter way.

CITV
http://www.citv.co.uk
Fun and games with all your favourite childrens ITV television shows in a nice colourful site.

Comedy Central
http://www.comcentral.com/
There's loads of stuff to download at this site as well as providing the opportunity to buy merchandise connected with its programmes, such as the fantastic South Park dolls!

Discovery *
http://www.discovery.com
This site runs in conjunction with the satellite channel of the same name, and very good it is too. As well as details of programmes, the site has loads of science and nature information. There's even a shop to buy stuff!

Dukes of Hazzard
http://hazzard.simplenet.com/
A whole host of links and information about Bo, Luke, Daisy, Rosco and good ol' Boss Hogg.

Friends
http://users.hunterlink.net.au/~dfdaj/
An unofficial Friends site which should answer any Friends related queries you may have. It won't, however, help you decide which one you fancy the most! Monica? Rachel? or maybe Chandler?

Futurama
http://www.foxworld.com/futurama
The official site of Matt Groenings latest cartoon sensation. The site provides profiles of the cast, a message board, and all the latest Futurama news.

Hollyoaks
http://www.hollyoaks.com/
Another of those TV companion sites. Not a huge amount here, but there is some gossip on the show's stars as well as updates.

Jerry Springer
http://www.universalstudios.com/tv/jerryspringer
Get up to date with goings on in the seediest and most talked about show around. Even suggest new topics for shows ("Honey, I'm sleeping with my Dreamcast"?)!

NBC

http://www.cbs.com
Perhaps the main focus for this site is
The Late Show with David Letterman.
Still going strong and still breaking new
ground, Letterman's best utterances are
reproduced here for all to marvel at.

Radio 1 *

http://www.bbc.co.uk/radio1
Containing all of the latest music and
entertainment news, plus the chance to
view schedules and playlists. The site
also provides webcams, where you get to
see the loveable Chris Moyles and co
doing their stuff in glorious Technicolor.
Best viewed in widescreen!

Red Dwarf

http://www.reddwarf.co.uk
Receive the latest news on the
adventures of Rimmer, Lister, Kryton, Cat
and co. Get the stories behind the crew
and plots, see below decks and
occasionally cyber chat with members of
the cast.

Scooby Doo *

http://www.scoobydoo.com/
A really fun site providing games and
activities for fans of the loveable canine
coward. Highlights include a create your
own Scooby snack contest, a colouring
corner and the haunted gameroom.

The Simpsons

http://www.foxworld.com/simpindx.htm
For any fans of The Simpsons, this is
worth a visit because it is very funny.

The Simpsons House

*http://www.lasvegassun.com/sun/dossier/
misc/simpsons/index.html*
Ever wanted to dive into your TV and
have a nose around the Simpsons
Springfield home? Now you can!

Sky

http://www.sky.co.uk
Although providing something of a
springboard to all its other channels, this
site works best when providing bang up
to date and well-written news and sport.

South Park *
http://www.beef-cake.com
The South Park information centre provides amazingly in depth information on the worlds favourite sick cartoon.

Talkback Productions
http://www.talkback.co.uk
One of the best production companies around at the moment, this site gives an early glimpse of any current projects as well as information about the company in general.

They Think It's All Over
http://www.talkback.co.uk/theythink/index.html
An official site for the often hilarious TV show. Bags of features and competitions await your visit.

Toaster
http://www.toaster.co.uk
A fairly basic but nonetheless useful site containing the entire TV and satellite channel programme listings available in this country.

Trouble
http://www.trouble.co.uk
If you're a regular watcher of this satellite kids channel then you couldn't ask for more. All the programmes are covered, plus games and competitions to have a try at.

Who Wants to be a Millionaire
http://www.phone-a-friend.com
Take a look behind the scenes of the UK's most popular quiz show. View the latest questions, check out the latest news and see pictures and interviews with the past winners.

Theatre and Performing Arts
• •

AWOL
http://www.execpc.com/~blankda/acting2.html
The Acting Workshop Online. Fascinating site for up and coming actors. Includes invaluable hints tips and advice ranging from basic stage roles to protecting yourself as an artist and making a living. Also contains an online bookshop.

British Actors Register

http://internet-ireland.ie/power/actor

Online showcase for British actors, aimed at agents/casting directors looking for British talent. Gender and alphabetical searches and links to other film and theatre resources. Artists registered include Rik Mayall and Brian Blessed.

Emmys

http://www.emmys.org

The Academy of Television Arts and Sciences. Everything you'll ever need to know about membership, members, and of course the prestigious awards themselves.

RADA

http://www.rada.org/

The Royal Academy of Dramatic Art. Details of courses offered, history of the organisation, student showcases and links to other sites including the Conference of Drama Schools.

The Royal Shakespeare Company

http://www.rsc.org.uk/

This official site updates you with upcoming productions, news, a box office where you can purchase tickets, and information about past and present performances.

Shakespeare *

http://www.shakespeare.org.uk/

The Shakespeare Birthplace Trust. Voted BBC radio 4's "personality of the millennium", Shakespeare's 'homepage' offers historical information, details of museums and houses, a library and an excellent diary of events.

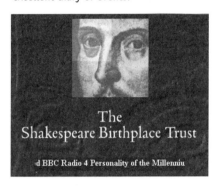

The Stage

http://www.thestage.co.uk/

The UK's only trade paper for theatre and television. Updated weekly, you can advertise your services online as well as view new production details and programme listings.

What's On Stage

http://www.whatsonstage.com/

Purchase tickets to the theatre, have a look at the latest theatre happenings around the country and take part in competitions.

Buddy - The Buddy Holly Story

http://www.mpcgroup.co.uk/buddy/

Carousel

http://www.shubert.com/carousel.html

Cats
http://www.reallyuseful.com/Cats/index.html

Doctor Dolittle
http://www.doctordolittle.co.uk/

Evita
http://www.thenewevita.com/

Grease
http://www.grease-tour.com

Les Miserables
http://www.lesmis.com/

Lord of the Dance
http://www.lordofthedance.com/

Mamma-Mia
http://www.mamma-mia.com/

Miss Saigon
http://www.miss-saigon.com/

Phantom Of the Opera
http://www.thephantomoftheopera.com/

Saturday Night Fever
http://www.nightfever.co.uk/

Transport

The AA *
http://www.theaa.co.uk/
This well presented site offers help and advice, registration details, facts about lead substitute petrol, European cover and basically everything to do with safe driving. Plus a comprehensive hotel search and booking facility.

Auto Trader
http://www.autotrader.co.uk/
Britains biggest source of used cars online. Search for registration numbers, cars and dealers, and advertise your own motor online. Includes a facility to search by make, model, price, age, and even how far you want to travel.

British School of Motoring
http://www.bsm.co.uk/
Information about learning to drive including a section about passing the theory test, with sample questions.

Carsource

http://carsource.co.uk/

Helpful page giving information on new and used cars in the UK. Offers buyers guides, finance help and an excellent search/request facility that links nationwide car dealers.

Hertz

http://www.hertz.co.uk/

Including an online booking service for cars all over the world. Also sections on heavy equipment rental and management information services.

Max Power

http://www.maxpower.co.uk/

The online version of the ultimate boy racers magazine. For enthusiasts of boomin' and cruisin'.

Official Mini Site

http://www.mini.co.uk

40 years of the Mini are celebrated with the full history. There is also a section for designing your own mini online, and some games.

RAC

http://www.rac.co.uk

Well designed site for the Royal Automobile Club. Features joining information, live updates on traffic problems, advice, and special offers.

Railtrack

http://www.railtrack.co.uk/

Providing online timetables and up to date train information for the UK.

Topcar.com

http://www.topcar.com/

An online magazine containing all that's new from the world of UK motoring.

Top Gear *

http://www.topgear.com

Online version of the Top Gear TV and magazine. Car reviews and features all in that inimitable Top Gear style.

Travel

1Ski

http://www.1ski.com/

Lots of skiing information in an easy to use format, which provides up to the minute details on any bargains as well as the all important snow reports.

Dreamcast travel

A2Btravel

http://www.a2btravel.com/
Flights, ferries, insurance, in fact
everything that you need travel-wise can
be found here. Use online mapping, find
out the lowdown on flight departure
delays or even book last minute bargains
with "the UK's biggest online travel
information and booking resource".

ATH

http://www.cs.cmu.edu/afs/cs/user/
mkant/Public/Travel/airfare.html
A complete online resource for
everything you will ever need for travel.
Flights, newsgroups, car hire, weather,
tourist information, health, languages,
currency, insurance, maps- the list goes
on. Essential viewing.

Are We Nearly There Yet?

http://www.indo.com/distance/
Calculate the distance between any two
cities, as the crow flies, with this nifty
longitude and latitude library. Great if
you have a helicopter!

Art of Travel

http://www.artoftravel.com/
A backpackers guide to seeing the world
on $25 a day or less. Written by an
experienced trekker this complete online
guide has tips, commentary and humour
for travellers of every kind.

B.A *

http:/www.british-airways.com/
Book online, view special offers, get
traveller's advice and find out about
world-wide airports at the home of
Concorde.

BAA

http://www.baa.co.uk/
Flying away to warmer climates in the
near future? Among many other
facilities, this site allows the traveller to
pre order their duty free selection and
collect when they arrive at the airport. It
also details the most hassle free way of
reaching BAA's UK airports.

Bargain Holidays *

http://www.bargainholidays.com/
Search an online database consisting of
over 70,000 late availability and
discounted holidays- even carry them
with you if you are lucky enough to own
a palm pilot!

Best of Ireland
http://www.iol.ie/~discover/
If you're curious about holidaying in
Ireland, this massive site is your answer.
As well as accommodation and
restaurants, the site has weather
forecasts, popular tourist attractions and
gig guides that cover the country. Some
lovely graphics are included here too,
which more than make up for the
sometimes dry text.

Britannia
http://www.britannia.com/
If you are travelling anywhere within the
UK, this site provides up to date travel
news and accommodation vacancies in
addition to numerous tourist hot spots.

British Foreign Office
http://www.fco.gov.uk/
Homepage of the Foreign and
Commonwealth office. This is essential
for travellers needing to ensure the
security of destinations or apply for
visas. Also featuring a handy "do's and
don'ts " for travellers and a dangerous
country blacklist.

Business Traveller Online
http://www.btonline.com
As the title suggests, this site is
designed to help the inexperienced
business traveller. The standard
information is included here – bars,
flights, places to eat and hotels, with
one eye always on your business
requirements.

Campus Travel
http://www.campustravel.co.uk
A site for all those students who
backpack thier way through the summer
break. Areas covered by the site include
cheap flights, InterRailing, American
flight passes and details on travelling to
and through the Andes.

Club 18-30
http://www.club18-30.co.uk/
A very eye catching site this one, but
also a bit on the slow side. Nevertheless
there's lively information on resorts,
hotels and big time partying in general.

Currency
http://www.oanda.com/
Over 150 major currencies are covered
here including the Euro. Get the latest
prices and exchange rates and find out
whether to hang on to that left over
holiday money.

Deckchair.Com

http://www.deckchair.com

Book flights in this easy to use no nonsense site. Set up to make booking flights on the internet as easy as possible. Great for checking prices in a hurry.

Discount Holidays and Flights

http://www.dedicate.co.uk/@uk/

Lots of attractive women pictured in this site, but it is actually very good. In depth information for budgeting your holiday plans. Car hiring, flights, hotels and local travel are all featured to help you on your way to a cheaper holiday.

Easyjet

http://www.easyjet.co.uk

Web site for the budget UK airline. Allows you to check times and availability of all Easyjet flights and provides secure on-line booking. Excellent stuff if you can travel out of Luton or Liverpool.

Ecotravel Centre

http://www.ecotour.org

A site for the environmentally friendly among you. Ecotravel Centre is dedicated to recommending holiday destinations and operators that are eco-friendly.

Expedia *

http://www.expedia.co.uk

On-line travel agent provided by Microsoft. Book flights, rooms and package holidays departing from the UK. Plus car rental, travel insurance and Last Minute deals.

Farebase Electronic

http://www.farebase.net/

This site will practically sort out your entire trip for you. Find a holiday, book a flight and find somewhere to stay by utilising the links it provides. Hire a car and you're sorted.

Go

http://www.go-fly.com

Go is British Airways' economy airline and this attractive looking site provides superb information for those of you wanting to go to Europe and the places to stay in when you arrive.

Infotel

http://www.infotel.co.uk

If you have found a low cost flight from one of the featured sites but still require somewhere to stay, this could be what you are looking for. The site will show what's available near you and will allow you to make a reservation.

Internet Holiday Rentals
http://www.holidayrentals.co.uk/
Photographs and descriptions of homes available for you to holiday in from all over the world. Some of the property is available to buy as well as rent.

Irish Tourist Board
http://www.ireland.travel.ie/
Have a look at some gorgeous scenery courtesy of the Irish Tourist Board. There's information on pubs here too, which is always a must.

ITS
http://www.itsnet.co.uk/
Internet Travel Services offers a comprehensive a to z of all things travel-wise. Travels, pilgrimages and weather are all covered along with a good last minute flight finder facility.

Last Minute
http://www.lastminute.com
Bargain last minute holidays in both the UK and abroad. Plus special late deals on flights and shows. Last minute deals are also auctioned to the highest bidder. Regular updates on late deals are sent to mailing list subscribers.

Loch Ness
http://www.ipw.com/lochness
Combine a holiday in beautiful Scotland with a little monster hunting. Check out this site if you want to find out how. Lots of pages including information on where to stay, travel and wildlife.

Loco Motives in Ibiza
http://www.housenation.com/loco-motives.htm
Ibiza offers some of the best clubs in the world. If fantastic DJs and fantastic venues are what you're after in a holiday take a trip to this site. Established now for 15 years, Loco Motives provides the best nights out and tells you how to get to and from the clubs, as well as offering discounts and free tickets.

Lonely Planet *
http://www.lonelyplanet.co.uk/
Lonely Planet publishes travel guides on places all over the globe. The site is great companion to the books. Look at

photos and get opinions from the people who have been there. Very extensive and simple to use.

National Express

http://www.nationalexpress.co.uk/
Book your long distance coach journey here. Review the fares and the timetables, and find services to major airports.

P&O Cruises

http://www.pocruises.com/
Reasonably good looking site giving you the ability to book your sailing on-line.

Piss up

http://www.piss-up.com
On-line travel agent specialising in cheap boozy citybreaks and heavy drinking festivals. Aimed mainly at students with pick-ups from university campuses throughout the UK.

Pontin's

http://www.pontins.com
A bright and breezy new interactive site ideal for searching for last minute bargains. Use the site to look for Golden Breaks for adults, Family Holidays, Special Interest Breaks and Island Holidays on Jersey and Ireland. Activity programmes are listed in the Family section and Special Offers are exactly that – last minute bargains.

Rough Guide

http://www.roughguides.com
A site that provides all the basic information you might need when choosing a destination and embarking on a holiday. Also provided is a section detailing the views of people who have been to the places included on the site.

Take Off!

http://www.takeoff.beeb.com/
Another impressive site from the BBC with detailed information on the more practical side of holidays. Find a destination from over 226 countries and take heed of the health care information provided.

The Worlds Most Dangerous Places

http://www.abcnews.com/sections/world/ dp/dp_intro.html
A site dedicated to the more dangerous places available for your holidays. This is not simply extreme sport but shooting in the streets. Very dangerous stuff. Take the bullet-proof vest not the sunscreen.

Thomson Holidays

http://www.thomson-holidays.com/
You can't actually book a holiday from this site, but it does provide examples of the sort of holidays available through its branches, as well as overseas job information.

Time Out

http://www.timeout.com
Web-site of the ever-popular weekly listings magazine. Contains regularly updated guides to the world's greatest cities, bars, clubs, hotels, restaurants, shops, galleries, museums and music venues. As well as the what's-on listings you will also find features, postcards, maps and classified ads.

Travlang

http://www.travlang.com
The travel and language supersite. Learn the basics for a host of foreign languages, make use of on-line translating dictionaries and book hotels all over the world.

Travelocity

http://www.travelocity.co.uk/
An amazingly comprehensive site, which really does have everything you need, (apart from sunshine), to get you well on your way to the perfect holiday. It even includes a handy currency converter.

UK Street Map

http://www.streetmap.co.uk/
A great way to plan your car journeys across the UK, this site has extensively researched road maps as well as a street map for London.

UK Travel Guide

http://www.uktravel.com
Everything you want to know about travel in the UK. Includes sections devoted to London and The Royal Family as well as a picture gallery, interactive map and on-line store.

Virgin *

http://www.fly.virgin.com/
A packed site home to the worlds 'other' favourite airline. Schedules, booking, travel tips and even a meeting place are all well set out and maintained.

Virtual Voyager

http://www.chron.com/voyager
If armchair holidaying is more your bag, the Virtual Voyager site will provide you

with some beautiful views in the comfort of your own home. Some of the views on offer include the Mardis Gras in New Orleans, Route 66 as well as the Texas Gulf Coast Hurricanes.

Wish You Were Here?

http://www.wishyouwerehere.com/
A companion site for the ITV holiday show. Like the TV show there are complaints, features on certain destinations and a huge section that covers almost the entire planet.

Weather

B.B.C Weather *

http://www.bbc.co.uk/weather
As with other BBC sites it's service is second to none. 24 hour and five day local forecasts, shipping news and world weather make this site an essential first port of call for short term weather information.

MET Office *

http://www.meto.gov.uk/
Forecasts, news, world links, research and more are all online here at the heart of the UK's favourite pastime.

The Weather Channel

http://www.weather.com/
Focussed mainly on the weather for America, this Internet version of the cable channel still contains weather forecasts on many regions of the United Kingdom, all displayed in Fahrenheit.

WMO

http://www.wmo.ch/
Point your browser towards the World Meteorological Organisation's website for a broader outlook on world weather, storms, climactic changes and weather systems.

World Climate Centre

http://www.worldclimate.com/
This site offers long-term weather predictions, in an easy to use city-based

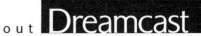
search engine. Giving average climate and precipitation figures to get an idea of the general state of affairs weather wise.

World-Wide-Weather

http://www.intellicast.com
With Intellicast's intuitive system you can view the world's weather with a bulletin posted every half an hour, and a cool radar tracking feature.

Weekends and Days Out

British Tourist Authority

http://www.visitbritain.com/frameset.htm
Official site, set up more for those visiting Britain than nationals, but lots of great information for everyone. The site looks great and the accommodation section is very thorough, with ratings and details on a huge number of places to stay.

Northern Ireland Tourist Board

http://www.ni-tourism.com
The official site. Good level of information on travel essentials in a clear and straightforward site. Ideal for planning a visit.

Scottish Tourist Board

http://www.holiday.scotland.net
Great looking official site. Lots of information including itineraries, accommodation, activities, and travel tips.

Welsh Tourist Board

http://www.visitwales.com
Not a great deal on this site. Links off to other sites to provide information. What it does is fine, but there is not much here.

Knowhere Guide to Britain

http://www.knowhere.co.uk
Great site with insider views of over 500 British towns. Can however be downbeat.

Alderney

http://www.alderney.gov.gg
Lots of photo's and a straightforward layout for the Island's tourist information. You can also email for a free brochure.

Guernsey
http://tourism.guernsey.net
All the usual travel information on this official tourist board site.

Jersey
http://www.jtourism.com
Clear site providing accommodation, what to see and do, travelling, and a brochure request form.

Places of Interest
British Waterways
http://www.british-waterways.org/
Official site covering boating, fishing, and canal holidays.

General information on the Lakes and the towns and villages of the region.

North Wales Tourism
http://www.nwt.co.uk/
Covers places of interest and accommodation. Information about Snowdonia is included.

Scottish Highlands
http://www.host.co.uk/
Great looking, slow loading. This official tourist board site covering accommodation, activities, events and even video footage.

English Riviera
http://www.torbay.gov.uk/tourism
Tourist information for Torbay, Paignton and Brixham. Simple layout and structure, but good for information.

Lake District
http://www.wwwebguides.com/britain/
cumbria/lakes/lakes.html

Stones of England
http://utenti.micronet.it/dmeozzi/
England/England.html
Covers ancient stone circles and the like with directions of how to get there.

Cities
Bath
http://www.bath.co.uk
A few problems with links within the site

not existing, but an interesting style to the site that is appealing.

Belfast
http://www.tourism.belfastcity.gov.uk
Clear and well laid out site with well presented information.

Blackpool
http://www.blackpool.gov.uk/btourism.htm
The official site, covering the usual facts, though not in huge detail. There is a free brochure request form though.

Bournemouth
http://www.bournemouth.co.uk
Unexciting with big lists of information. Very text heavy but simplistic.

Brighton
http://www.brighton.co.uk
Fine presentation, with restaurant reviews, accommodation guide and attractions. Lots of good maps and information on travelling.

Cardiff
http://www.cardiff.gov.uk.
Official site including accommodation, places of interest and travel information. You do have to hunt around for it though!

Chester
http://www.chestercc.gov.uk/tourism/home.htm
Official government site that covers the standard travel information in a clear way.

Edinburgh
http://www.edinburgh.org
Official site covering the important travel information. Plus useful links to anything that the site does not cover.

Glasgow
http://www.glasgow.uk.com/
Tourist information, accommodation, maps and even a web-cam. Basic site design.

Liverpool
http://www.merseyside.org.uk
Very heavy style to the site, which is interesting but annoying to navigate if you just want the facts.

London
http://www.londontown.com
Official great looking site. Loads really slowly, but it does have excellent

presentation. Accommodation, dining, attractions, pubs, maps and shopping.

Manchester

http://www.manchesteronline.co.uk/guide
Part of the Manchester Online site covering the usual tourist essentials.

Newquay

http://www.newquay.org.uk/
Good site covering accommodation, the beaches and surfing. Includes an online brochure request form.

Oxford

http://www.oxfordcity.co.uk/
Very good site covering the city, with a great accommodation section and a smart clear layout.

York

http://www.thisisyork.co.uk/
Published by the Evening Press paper this site covers all tourism issues along with much more.

Theme Parks

Alton Towers

http://www.alton-towers.co.uk
Examine the rides, find out about pricing, see what special events are on, find out how to get there, and get tips to make the most of the park.

American Adventure

http://www.adventureworld.co.uk/
Covers the attractions, special events, and admission prices. Plain, but effective.

Blackpool Pleasure Beach

http://www.bpbltd.com/
Stylish official park site. Details of the park, tickets, events and shows. You may have to click on the non-java menu on the opening screen to view it though!

Chessington World of Adventure

http://www.users.globalnet.co.uk/~rpd/chess/
This unofficial site covers all you will need in a clear well presented manner.

Lots of good ride photos to!

Drayton Manor

http://www.drayton-manor.co.uk
Clear layout covers prices, location, and general park information.

Great Yarmouth Pleasure Beach

http://www.pleasure-beach.co.uk/ frameset.htm
Unexciting site contains pricing information, photo's and location information

Lego Land

http://www.legoland.co.uk/
Lego feeling site with all the ride, show, special event and booking information neatly presented. You can even book tickets online.

Longleat

http://www.longleat.co.uk/
Lots of information on pricing and getting to the park. Nothing on the animals though.

Thorpe Park

http://www.thorpepark.co.uk
Simple site that covers the major rides, pricing and location of the park. The site is not the easiest to navigate due to the odd headings such as Mums and Dads instead of ticket pricing.

Glossary

· ·

Attachment   A File sent with an Email.

AOL   America Online. An international content provider.

AVI   Microsoft's famous compressed video format.

Bandwidth   The size of a data connection which carries Internet traffic. More bandwidth means more possible traffic at any given time.

BBS   Bulletin Board System. What people used before the Internet hit the mainstream. The poor fools.

Bookmarks   Netscape's way of keeping a list of your favourite Web sites.

Browser   A program used to browse the World Wide Web.

Cookie   Small text file which sites can store on your computer so that when you return to the site it already knows your information.

Cracker   Somebody who hacks into computers with malicious intent. Also somebody who breaks the copy protection on commercial software for distribution in pirate channels.

Domain name   An Internet address, such as Altavista.com.

Download   Transfer a file from a machine on the Internet to your own computer.

Dreamkey   The software you use to access the Internet

DreamArena   The main Dreamcast Website - your home on the Internet.

Email   Electronic Mail.

FAQ   Frequently Asked Questions. An explanatory text file put together by somebody who is fed up of answering the same questions over and over again.

Flame   An angry/abusive attack on somebody in a Newsgroup.

FTP   File Transfer Protocol.

GUI   (Pronounced 'gooey') Graphical User Interface. A means of using software through the mouse rather than, for example, the keyboard.

Hacker	Somebody who 'breaks in' to computers on the Internet.
Half-life	Extremely popular online game.
Header	The beginning of an Email message which is concerned with the addressing and the identity of the sender.
HTML	Hypertext Markup Language. The language of the World Wide Web. All Web pages are written in HTML.
HTTP	HyperText Transfer Protocol. The protocol for web communications.
IP Address	A series of numbers which designate the unique location of each computer on the Internet.
ISDN	Integrated Services Digital Network. The standard for digital telephone communication. Allows Internet access at 12k per second, if you can afford it.
ISP	Internet Service Provider. Your gateway to the Internet. Most of these are free services, you just pay local call rates to connect to them.
Java	A program language that is designed to produce programs which should, in theory, be able to run on almost any modern operating system.
JPEG	The most-used picture format on the Internet. Allows high amounts of compression. It is a *lossy* format - this means that the better the compression, the worse the image quality.
Lamer	Rude term for somebody who is either computer illiterate or simply stupid.
LAN	Local Area Network. An independent network, which may or may not be connected to the Internet.
MIDI	Musical Instrument Digital Interface. In the context of online use, MIDI files contain information for synthesizers. Computers can play these files too, however, and they take up only a minute amount of disk space. Sometimes only a few Kilobytes for five minutes of music. Sound quality is often akin to that of a 1980s electronic organ, unfortunately. MIDI files are often (far too often) used as background music on Web pages.
MP3	The MPEG format for storing sound files. CD quality sound can be stored at around one Megabyte per minute of audio.
MPEG	One of the most popular forms of compressed video files.

Netiquette   The way one should conduct oneself on the internet.

Newbie   Somebody who is new to using the Internet or a particular aspect of it.

Newsgroups   The world's biggest bulletin board system. Works in conjunction with Email.

NNTP   The standard for dealing with Newsgroup postings.

Ping   A program used to check if a host is available, or how fast it is relative to your location.

Plugin   A file used to upgrade or work with another program, such as a Web browser.

POP3   Post Office Protocol. The most often used format for Email servers.

Proxy   A proxy is an invisible server that sits between you and the Internet, and it downloads files that you request and then sends them to you. They're usually used to act like a cache - they store previously downloaded Web pages on them that will be sent to you whenever you request that Web site. Sometimes they are used to monitor or control Internet sites visited.

Search Engine   A huge searchable database of Web sites. They usually use programs called 'Robots' to seek out and list all of the Web sites they can find.

Server   A machine on the Internet used to make information or services available to people.

SMTP   Simple Mail Transfer Protocol. A type of server used by many ISPs to send users email.

Smiley   An emotive symbol used to express humour or sadness when chatting or using Newsgroups. For example, :-) is happy, and :-(is sad. You have to imagine them turned 90 degrees clockwise to see how they work.

Spam   Junk Email, named Spam after a Monty Python sketch. Sadly, Spam is not yet illegal. Almost all Spam mails contain information concerning illegal scams, however. Never, ever buy anything advertised via an unsolicited email.

Surfing   The media friendly term for using the internet.

Telnet   Allows you to log into remote computers. Used for direct computer access and talkers.

Troll   Somebody who delights in causing controversy or getting on people's nerves. Usually refers to Newsgroup posters.

UNIX   A very old and largely text-based Operating System, still used by most serious Internet users (such as large businesses and most or all ISPs).

URL Uniform Resource Locator. A Web address.

Virus Hidden programs which can corrupt your software.

VM The memory unit for the Dreamcast, used to hold saved games and special VM games.

Web site A collection of documents published on the Internet.

WWW World Wide Web. A huge network of documents, consisting of text, graphics, sound and video. The World Wide Web is not the Internet - just a part of it.

WYSIWYG What You See Is What You Get. How you see something on screen is the way it will really turn out.

Abbreviations & Smileys

AFAIK	-	As Far As I Know
AFK	-	Away From Keyboard
ASAP	-	As Soon As Possible
ATM	-	At The Moment
BBS	-	Be Back Soon
BBL	-	Be Back Later
BF	-	Boyfriend
BRB	-	Be Right Back
BTW	-	By The Way
CU	-	See You
FFS	-	For ('flips') Sake
FYI	-	For Your Information
GDI	-	God Damn It
GF	-	Girlfriend
IMHO	-	In My Humble Opinion
IRL	-	In Real Life
KB	-	Keyboard
LOL	-	Laughs/Laughing Out Loud
PPL	-	People
RL	-	Real Life
ROFL	-	Rolls On the Floor Laughing
ROTFL	-	Rolls On The Floor Laughing
RTFM	-	Read the Flipping (!) Manual
TIA	-	Thanks In Advance
TTFN	-	Ta Ta For Now
WTF	-	What/Who/Where/When The Flip (!)
WWW	-	World Wide Web

Often in chat, emotives have to be expressed in the form of smileys. Emotion can't always be read into normal text, and smileys can prevent people from taking sarcastic comments seriously. Turn the book on it's side to turn the following characters into smiley (or otherwise!) faces.

206

:-)	-	Smiling
;-)	-	Winking. Used when joking etc.
;-P	-	Tongue out
;-P~	-	Tongue out and dribbling
:-D	-	A big teethy smile!
:-S	-	Oops!
:-/	-	Can mean glum, unsure, sceptical, sighing etc.
:-(	-	Sad
:~(	-	Crying
:-)))	-	Very happy.
:-0	-	Shouting
>:-)	-	Devious

Internet Facts

- Internet usage is increasing by over 200% a year.

- In 1998, Internet business activity was to the tune of $300 billion. Now, it makes more money than the car industry.

- Internet companies account for 40% of the total increase in employment.

- There were 100 million people online at the end of 1997, most of which were in the United States.

- 40 per cent of online shopping takes place between 10pm and 10am.

- Over 25 per cent of all homes will be connected to the Internet by 2001.

- Online auctioneer eBay has 1.5 billion hits a month and 2,568 different categories.

-In October 1999, Gordon Brown made a speech at the UK Internet Summit, in which he said 'Thirty years ago this month the Internet was invented in Britain'. Of course, it was invented in the USA.

- Internet users over the age of 17:
        6 million people have made purchases online.
        17 million households are online.
        58% are male; 42% are female.
        40.3% have professional or managerial careers
        Internet Use is split between personal (45%), business (33%), education (16%) and other (6%)
        45.70% are married.

-Only 50 million Europeans are online, compared to 115 million in the US and Canada.

- A mere 1.72 million are online in Africa. The grand total is thought to be something in the region of 200 million.

- Online spending in the UK is predicted to rise by 1000% before 2002, with an estimated £1940 million being spent that year.

Internet & Game Jokes

One major benefit to being online is the amount of stupid lists, jokes, stories and other bizarre rubbish that you will find yourself receiving onm email. Friends, colleagues and just about anyone else you can think of will send you such things as:

Top Ten Signs You are an Internet addict

1.   When filling out your driver's license application you give your IP address.
2.   You no longer ask prospective dates what their sign is, instead your line is "Hi, what's your URL?"
3.   Instead of calling you to dinner, your spouse sends e-mail.
4.   You're amazed to find out spam is a food.
5.   You "ping" people to see if they're awake, "finger" them to find out how they are, and "AYT" them to make sure they're listening to you.
6.   When you go on an organised tour you check if the transportation is ethernet, fibre-optics or token ring.
7.   You introduce your wife as "my lady@home.wife"
8.   At social functions you introduce your husband as "my domain server".
9.   You think that :-) is your mirror image.10. Your name is "anonymous"

Everything I need to know I have learnt from Video Games

1.   There is no problem that cannot be overcome by violence.
2.   You can overcome most adversaries simply by having enough change.
3.   If it moves, KILL IT!
4.   Operating any vehicle or weapon is simple and requires no training.
5.   "Bosses" always hire henchmen weaker than they are to do their dirty work.
6.   If you find food lying on the ground, eat it.
7.   You can smash things and get away with it because:
     a. Smashing things doesn't hurt.
     b. Many nice things are hidden inside other things.
8.   When someone dies, they disappear.
9.   Money is frequently found lying on the streets.
10. All shopkeepers carry high-tech weaponry.
11. You never run out of bullets, only grenades.

12. Ninjas are common, and fight in public frequently.

13. Whenever huge evil fat men are about to die, they begin flashing red or yellow.

14. When you are born, you're invulnerable for a brief period of time.

15. Although the enemy always has more aircraft than you, they fly in predictable patterns which makes it easier for you to shoot them all down.

16. All women wear revealing clothing and have great bodies.

17. The enemy always leaves weapons and ammo laying around for no other reason than so their bitter enemies can pick them up and defeat them with it.

18. You sustain injury if you shoot innocents.

19. Gang members frequently all look the same, and often have the same names.

20. When driving, do not worry if your vehicle crashes and explodes. A new one will appear in its place.

Know the Score!

If you would like information on FKB Publishing's future releases please fill
in the form below (or a photocopy) and send it to:

FKB Publishing Ltd.
Ref. DCIG
Wellpark
Willeys Avenue
Exeter
EX2 8BE
United Kingdom

Name

Address

Postcode

What is your favourite Dreamcast Game?

Your Age?

12 or under ☐   13-17 ☐   18-24 ☐   25+ ☐

Where did you buy this book?

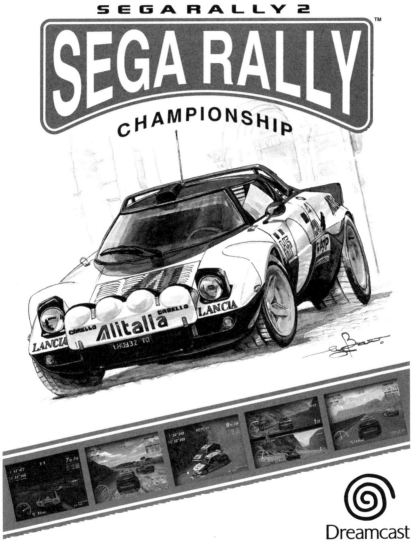

SEGA RALLY 2

SEGA RALLY
CHAMPIONSHIP
™

Dreamcast

Up to 6 billion players
www.dreamcast-europe.com

SONIC™ ADVENTURE

SONIC TEAM PRESENTS

Dreamcast
Up to 6 billion players
www.dreamcast-europe.com

2000 uk edition

definitive
guide to internet
travel

FKB
publishing

the definitive travel guide using the internet

only
£7.99